THE GARDEN COOK

Grow, Cook and Eat with Kids

FIONA INGLIS

MURDOCH BOOKS

While she was a MasterChef Australia contestant, Fiona Inglis confessed she wanted to become involved in the Stephanie Alexander Kitchen Garden program. Subsequently she became an inspiring and well-loved teacher in the program operating at Findon Primary School and three years later has written this excellent book. Drawing on her real-life experience of working with primary school-aged children she has produced a lively book that covers all aspects of cooking and gardening, including plenty of helpful advice and recipes. The book is written in simple, clear language, is beautifully illustrated and is guaranteed to appeal to all young cooks and gardeners (and to inspire their parents).

STEPHANIE ALEXANDER

CONTENTS

FIONA'S FAVOURITES

My favourite herbs are basil and thyme...
I love the sweetness and freshness of basil when it's in season.
It makes summer feel so special. Thyme, on the other hand, is
available nearly all year round and complements many different
foods, such as chicken, meat and most vegetables.

FOR KIDS

Once upon a time there was a fussy little girl named Fiona. She pushed her food around the plate, refused to eat certain vegetables and showed minimal interest in what food was, let alone where it came from. Is it hard to believe? I'm sorry to say it's true, my love for fresh food was slow to develop. As a child I knew little about the magical way a veggie patch springs to life and I wasn't really encouraged to cook on a daily basis. Now, I am making up for lost time.

I have realised that the best way to learn about food is through experience. It is about getting your hands a little bit dirty, with soil in the garden and flour in the kitchen! I hope you enjoy this joyous and memorable food journey as much as I've enjoyed sharing it. I only wish I had discovered it sooner.

FOR PARENTS

I am a primary school teacher from Victoria working in one of Stephanie Alexander's influential Kitchen Garden programs. The aim of the program is to take children on a fabulous food journey, inspiring them to discover the fun and flavours of the kitchen and garden. Children are encouraged to taste healthy foods (happily!) and develop lifelong skills. Cooking regularly allows them to experience new tastes, textures, smells and flavours, building the framework for a healthy lifestyle. The ultimate goal is to positively influence children's food choices and help them connect with the world around us.

This cookbook is the culmination of the experience I have gained from the classroom and my love of cooking with children. Fresh, engaging and exciting, it is centered around the philosophy that food should be explored early in life. By encouraging children to experience growing and preparing food, healthy eating will naturally take its place in their lives. Allowing children to explore a wide variety of foods leads to a deeper appreciation and understanding of them.

It's easy to underestimate children's willingness to learn. Every day I am amazed at my students' observations, engagement and growing interest in food and its environment. They learn how to grow and enjoy seasonal organic food, free from packaging and processing. We explore food from seed to harvest, preparation to plate. We plant, water and nurture our environment in order to achieve the best possible product. My students monitor the garden intently, asking questions such as 'When should these seeds be planted?' and 'Is this ripe enough to pick?' We experience food from the roots up and they learn lifelong practical skills.

I can't help but smile when I hear a student say something like 'I never liked tomato before today' or 'I hate beetroot, but I like beetroot risotto.' I love the way children may scrunch up their faces in disgust as they taste something new, but then gobble it up happily the following week because it's prepared in a slightly different way. When I sit with my students at our kitchen table to eat the meals we have created, everybody tries them because they understand the effort that has gone into growing and preparing the ingredients. There is always great excitement, celebration and pride in the dishes.

I hope this book encourages children's natural desire to learn. By engaging and connecting with real food, they will be empowered to make their own decisions about what they eat. Involving children in the production of food, from start to finish, sets a strong foundation for healthy eating and sustainable living. I hope you embrace the message of GROW, COOK and EAT; discover the wonderful world of food with your children and enjoy the health and happiness it brings!

BASICS

Before we embark on our cooking adventures it is important we understand some simple kitchen strategies and plan ahead a little. This chapter features important safety tips, a helpful glossary and other useful information to ensure your cooking runs smoothly. As usual, the more practice you have, the better the results will be. My golden kitchen rules are:

* Ask questions, because that is the
best way to learn.
* It's okay to make mistakes.
* Take your time, read the recipe first and
enjoy cooking with others.
* Always wash your hands before cooking —
good hygiene makes a healthy cook!
* Ask an adult to help you when using sharp
knives, the stovetop or oven.

COOKING EQUIPMENT

At our school, I encourage my students to keep a checklist of handy kitchen equipment and tools for their cooking areas. You don't need to have every piece of equipment on this list, but it is a useful guide. You might enjoy collecting handy nick-nacks for the kitchen, like I do — my favourite piece of equipment is a baby whisk, shaped like a flower at one end!

- **Mixing bowls** are used nearly all the time. I suggest an assortment of sizes and at least one that is heatproof.

- **Peeler** to remove the skin of vegetables and some fruits.

- **Measuring cups** to measure quantities of ingredients. They usually come in a set of four: ⅓, ¼, ½ and 1 cup measurements. Always level off the measuring cup with your finger so it is flat and not heaped.

- **Sieve/sifter** to sift dry ingredients, strain liquids or remove solids from mixtures.

- **Colander** to strain liquid, rinse fruits and vegetables, and drain pasta.

- **Grater** to shred cheese, vegetables or fruits.

- **Microplane grater** for very finely mincing garlic or ginger, or grating parmesan cheese. It is also great for removing the zest of citrus fruits.

- **Measuring jug** for measuring liquids such as water, stock, cream, and so on in millilitres (ml/fl oz). A handle is essential for pouring liquids easily.

- **Measuring spoons** for measuring small quantities of ingredients. They often come in a set with ¼ teaspoon, ½ teaspoon, 1 teaspoon and 1 tablespoon. Always level off the spoon with your finger so it is flat and not heaped.

- **Whisks** have long, narrow wire loops and are used for whisking eggs, mixing dressings and mixing sauces so they are free of lumps.

- **Wooden spoons** are used to stir ingredients. They do not transmit heat.

- **Ladles** are large, deep spoons with a long handle, great for serving soups or sauces.

- **Tongs** are used to pick up ingredients, especially when hot, and serve food such as pasta or barbecued meats.

- **Slotted spoons** are large spoons with holes in them and a long handle. Good for straining pasta and gnocchi or removing cooked food from a deep fryer.

- **Pastry brush** for brushing pastry with egg, milk or oil.

- **Spatulas** are flat with a long handle made from silicone, plastic or rubber. They are great for stirring, folding and (if silicone) turning food when frying.

- **Juicer** for extracting juice from citrus fruits. There is usually a rim to collect the pips, keeping them out of the juice.

- **Thin metal skewers** to test if cakes are ready. Insert one into the centre of the cake and if it comes out clean, the cake is cooked.

- **Rolling pins** are long cylinders with handles, usually made of wood, used to roll out doughs and pastry so they are flattened for pizzas, pies and tarts.

- **Scales** to weigh ingredients in grams/ ounces. Most scales have a 'Tare' button that comes in handy if you place a bowl on the scales but don't want to measure it. Press 'Tare' to return the scales to 0, then measure the ingredients.

- **Food processors** are used to process, pulse, mix, grate, chop and even juice ingredients. There are many varieties with different capabilities. I always make my pasta dough and shortcrust pastry in the food processor.

- **Electric mixer** for whisking egg whites into soft or stiff peaks, mixing cake batters and whipping cream. You can get hand-held mixers or those on a stand with a bowl attachment.

- **Blender** for making smoothies, shakes and other drinks, as well as purées and blending soups.

- **Saucepans** are round, deep and heatproof with high sides and long handles, essential for cooking on the stovetop. Have an assortment of sizes.

- **Woks** are large, deep heatproof pans used for stir-frying, and sometimes deep-frying, on the stovetop.

- **Frying pans** are flat, round heatproof pans with long handles, essential for frying or sautéing on the stovetop. Have an assortment of sizes.

- **Serving spoons** are large spoons with long handles used for serving portions of food, such as short pastas, rice, stews and curries.

- **Dessertspoons** for tasting dishes as you cook. This is very important, particularly before and after seasoning dishes with salt and pepper.

- **Bakeware** such as trays, muffin tins, tart (flan) tins and cake tins (including spring-form). A selection of non-stick bakeware will ensure your baking is a success. Silicone bakeware, which doesn't heat up like metal does, is also available at cookware stores.

- **Ruler** for measuring tins and pastry.

- **Scissors** for cutting baking paper to size.

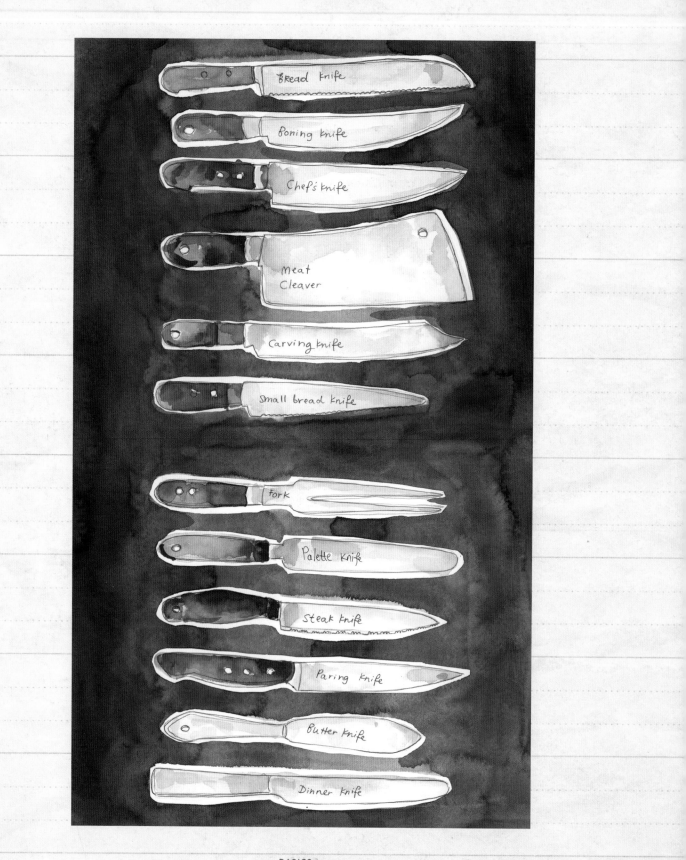

KNIFE SAFETY

- Always hold a knife by the handle. Hold it by your side and pointing to the floor when transporting it around the room.

- Always chop on a flat surface. Cut round-shaped food such as onions, apples, oranges and so on in half, then turn them cut-side-down so they are stable when chopping.

- Keep little fingers tucked in and don't be afraid to ask for assistance from an adult if you need help.

- Choose the right-sized knife for the appropriate food. For example, when chopping pumpkin or potatoes use a larger knife. For smaller foods such as mushrooms and tomatoes, use a smaller knife (possibly a serrated one).

- It is important to place your chopping board and knife at a level that is right for you so you have a clear view and feel comfortable. If you are little, you may need to stand on a sturdy stool. Place a damp tea towel (dish towel) under the chopping board to prevent it moving.

- Never wave a knife around and always place it to one side of the chopping board when it's not being used. Don't drop a knife into soapy water and walk away, as you may cut yourself on it later.

- A mandoline is a very sharp cooking utensil used for slicing and cutting fruits and vegetables. It comes with suitable attachments or blades to achieve very thin slices, julienne strips or crinkle-cuts. A mandoline will always have a safety guard attachment, which is used to slide the piece of food along the blade to cut. Never try to cut food using your hands only as mandolines are extremely sharp. Make sure the food is put on the guard handle and ask an adult to help you. Always ask an adult to clean the mandoline when you are finished — we don't want any cut fingers!

TEASPOON AND TABLESPOON CONVERSIONS

¼ teaspoon = 1.25 ml

½ teaspoon = 2.5 ml

1 teaspoon = 5 ml

1 tablespoon = 20 ml (½ fl oz)

CUP CONVERSIONS

¼ cup = 60 ml (2 fl oz)

⅓ cup = 80 ml (2½ fl oz)

½ cup = 125 ml (4 fl oz)

¾ cup = 185 ml (6 fl oz)

1 cup = 250 ml (9 fl oz)

1¼ cups = 310 ml (10¾ fl oz)

2½ cups = 625 ml (21½ fl oz)

5 cups = 1.25 litres (44 fl oz)

20 cups = 5 litres (175 fl oz)

1 Always use a measuring jug with clearly marked measurements on the side for liquid quantities.

FULL-CREAM MILK

2 See-through plastic or glass is best.

3 A set of standard individual measuring spoons and cups is also handy for both dry and liquid ingredients.

½ cup   ¾ cup   1 cup

4 Scales are useful for measuring dry ingredients by weight (grams or ounces).

BASICS

USING THE STOVETOP AND OVEN

When using the stovetop and oven, it is important to remember that this is where fires can start in the kitchen. Here are some simple safety tips to ensure you cook in a safe environment. It is okay to burn food — I have done it a million times! But it is not okay to burn yourself. I'd rather have black brownies than a nasty burn.

- Ask an adult friend or family member to help whenever you need to use the oven or stovetop.

- Always wear oven mitts or heat-protective material when removing hot dishes from the oven or stovetop.

- Always keep the long handles of pans and woks to the side of the stovetop to avoid them being knocked over.

- Never leave a hot stovetop unattended.

- Always keep oven areas clear of plastic, glass, paper or highly flammable materials, such as aerosols, as these can cause fires.

- Always use appropriate-sized heatproof pans and bakeware.

- Place hot pans on heatproof mats, not straight on the bench. Also, warn people when transporting hot foods or moving around — a quick shout of 'hot dish behind you' works well.

DEEP-FRYING

Deep-frying is not a cooking technique for every day, as it is not the healthiest form of cooking. However, it gives delicious results and is fine for every now and then. Always follow these simple safety procedures to avoid accidents.

- Ask an adult friend or family member to assist you at all times.

- Half-fill a medium saucepan or wok with vegetable or canola oil and place on the stovetop. Heat over low heat and never leave it unattended.

- Heat the oil to the temperature specified in the recipe. If you don't have a thermometer, a good way to test if the oil is hot enough is to drop a cube of bread in it — the recipes will tell you how long it should take to turn brown. Or, you can place the handle of a wooden spoon in the oil and if it starts to bubble up around the handle, it is ready for frying.

- Never place fingers or any other body part in hot oil and don't stand too close when frying. Don't drop food into the oil from a great height, as this can cause splatters of hot oil that may burn you. Lower the food in gently or ask an adult to do it for you. If you are adding something that is battered or not entirely dry, be extra careful as it will splatter when it goes into the oil.

- Fry small portions of food in batches, say 3–4 at a time. Adding too much food in one go will lower the temperature of the oil.

- Use a slotted spoon (a large spoon with holes in it) or tongs to remove cooked food from hot oil and always drain it on paper towels.

- Don't pour oil down the sink. Allow it to cool, then dispose of it in the bin.

HELPFUL GLOSSARY OF COOKING TERMS

- **Beat** To whisk with force, by hand or using an electric mixer. This can thicken ingredients such as cream or transform runny egg whites into snowy peaks.

- **Cream** To combine sugar and butter by beating with an electric mixer on medium speed until light, fluffy and pale. Always use room-temperature unsalted butter, chopped into small cubes. The sugar needs to be thoroughly mixed with the butter.

- **Whisk** To combine ingredients using a whisk until the desired consistency.

- **Fold** Using a silicone spatula or large spoon, gently scrape around the outside of the bowl and cut through the centre of the mixture several times. This is a gentle process to combine ingredients and maintain air in the mixture.

- **Sauté** To fry ingredients in a frying pan or saucepan (usually with a little oil or butter), stirring with a wooden spoon.

- **Process** Using a food processor to cut and combine one or more ingredients to the desired consistency.

Pulse A setting on a food processor that chops and combines ingredients in short bursts, only while the button is pressed. This is a good way to mix ingredients gradually.

Purée To blend ingredients until smooth, usually with a stick blender or electric blender.

Combine To mix ingredients together using a wooden spoon or spatula until incorporated evenly.

Knead Shape the dough into a ball. On a clean, floured bench, use the heel of your (clean) hand to push hard on the dough while pulling it towards you with the other hand, turning and folding it over frequently. Kneading can take up to 10 minutes — always check your recipe.

Strain Placing ingredients in a sieve or colander to remove excess liquid.

HERB GUIDE

Herbs are wonderful plants, full of flavour, that bring food to life. I don't think I could cook successfully without them! They are beautiful, fragrant and easy to grow. Here is a simple herb guide to help you identify and cook with them. Always be delicate when handling fresh herbs as they bruise easily and the perfume can be squeezed out if they are handled too roughly. When chopping delicate herbs, do it gently and quickly. Basil is best simply torn, as it blackens after chopping with a metal blade.

Rosemary

Sage I love this fragrant pale-green herb, especially teamed with pumpkin or pork.

Rosemary A popular, robust herb with tough, spike-like leaves. It is great for roasting foods, such as potatoes and lamb. Adding rosemary to oils to flavour them also works a treat. I love adding it to fresh bread or pizza dough.

Sage

Chives This member of the onion family has a very mild onion taste. It is long and grass-like, and is great in salads or with fish.

Oregano

chives

Mint A zesty, refreshing herb that grows very well (sometimes too well!) in the garden. It is great in salads, stir-fries and soups or sprinkled over lamb.

mint

Oregano can come in many varieties and grows year-round. It has an earthy flavour and is used in many Italian and Greek dishes. It works well in pastas, on pizzas or in tomato-based sauces, marinades for meat and dressings for salads.

Bay
Leaves

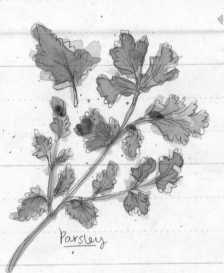

Parsley

Bay leaves are tough green leaves that come from a tree and can be dried whole. They are commonly used to flavour slow-cooked dishes such as bolognese sauce, soups and stews. Always remove them before serving.

Parsley Comes in two varieties; curly or flat-leaf (Italian/continental). I generally use flat-leaf parsley, as I think it has a better flavour. Parsley works with nearly everything from red meats to poultry, fish, salads, grains/pulses and pastas.

Basil This sweet, delicate herb has a large, vibrant green leaf. It highlights the summer season and works brilliantly with tomatoes, soft cheeses and pasta.

Basil

coriander

Coriander (cilantro) One of my favourite herbs, coriander has a strong, distinctive flavour. It is used widely in Asian dishes (especially Thai), as well as Middle Eastern food and some curries.

Thyme A lovely herb that also comes in many varieties and can have a small purple flower. It is great with red meats, poultry, pastas and vegetables such as beans, mushrooms and leeks. It is also good for marinades and stuffings.

Thyme

GROW

EQUIPMENT

Planting a veggie patch is easy and immensely
rewarding. Growing vegetables, herbs and fruits from
scratch helps us appreciate the journey they
have made to get onto our plates.

WHAT SHOULD I GROW?

When planting your herbs and vegetables, it is important to choose a mixture of good-quality soil, fertiliser, compost and natural materials such as lucerne or straw. I like to layer them – one layer on top of the next. Top it all off with a bag of worm poo to enrich your soil with good nutrients and you are ready to go!

If this is your first veggie patch, my advice would be to start small. I began with a selection of herbs and when I felt confident about them, I moved onto some favourite, easy-to-grow recipe staples — lettuce, spring onions (scallions), tomatoes and so on. Choose plants that suit your soil and the weather conditions in your area, and that you know you will use and eat! There is no point planting unusual vegetables, herbs and fruits that you have no interest in eating.

Cabbage

Leek

Basil

Broccoli

COMPOST LAYER

SOIL

FERTILISER

STRAW

HOW TO SET UP A HERB GARDEN OR VEGGIE PATCH

Creating an edible garden is achievable for everyone, regardless of how much space is available. Even a balcony or windowsill can produce great results with plants in pots. Follow these simple steps to make your perfect patch.

- Choose a suitable area. Make sure it receives plenty of sunlight.

- Choose your material. You could try a raised garden bed made from timber, a ready-made planter box or container/tub, half a large wine barrel (you may need to seal the inside), or you may simply want to use a patch of grass. Steer clear of unsealed terracotta pots as they can suck up too much water, starving the plants.

- If using a planting tray, fill it to a depth of at least 15 cm (6 inches) with seed-raising mix and make sure there are good drainage holes. Add good-quality compostable layers to the soil as they will break down and feed your plants as they grow. Some examples are compost, slow-release organic fertiliser (in pallet form), plain straw or lucerne hay.

- Choose a selection of seasonal seeds/seedlings to sow or plant, making sure they'll encourage and complement each other while growing.

● Level your soil and sow your selected seeds or seedlings in rows, leaving at least 4 cm (1½ inches) between each. If you are using seedlings in punnets, gently remove them from their containers and tickle the roots with your fingers to loosen them slightly before planting. Make sure your seeds and seedlings are covered with soil mix and are nicely packed in, with any leaves fully exposed.

● Give your seeds a good watering. Freshly sown seeds need to be kept quite moist until they germinate or sprout.

● Once your seeds have grown into seedlings around 10 cm (4 inches) tall, you can mulch around the growing area with lucerne. At this point they can be transported to a larger area if necessary.

● Create a simple compost bin in your garden to provide nutritious, rich organic matter to scatter over your new veggie patch. Get into the habit of saving discarded food scraps, paper or old garden matter to put in your compost bin.

● Be patient. You will need to allow 2–4 months growing time, depending on the type of plant. If you are planting seeds, they will take slightly longer than seedlings.

SPRING AND SUMMER HARVEST BOXES

Spring and summer are tremendous times for growth and some really exciting vegetables, fruits and herbs are harvested in the warmer months. Start preparing and planting around August and September.

Always remember you need to plan ahead when planting for the next season.

IDEAS FOR SPRING AND SUMMER HARVEST BOXES
- Basil
- Capsicums (peppers)
- Cucumbers
- Eggplant (aubergines)
- Lettuce
- Oregano
- Strawberries
- Thyme
- Tomatoes

AUTUMN AND WINTER HARVEST BOXES

The cooler months bring plenty of tasty offerings, too. For autumn and winter harvest boxes, prepare and plant from March through to June or July.

IDEAS FOR AUTUMN AND WINTER HARVEST BOXES
- Broad (fava) beans
- Broccoli
- Cabbage
- Chives
- English spinach
- Kale
- Rainbow chard
- Silverbeet (Swiss chard)

Jennifer, 9

Vaughn, 10

WHY IS FRESH, SEASONAL FOOD BEST?

Eating food when it is in season means you are enjoying it when it is at its peak, when it is ripe and ready to be picked from the trees or pulled from the ground. Certain temperatures and weather conditions are required for the ripening process, and these vary depending on the fruit or vegetable. For example, apples are generally ready to harvest in autumn while strawberries ripen over summer. There are a number of reasons why it is best to use local seasonal produce, including superior flavour and less impact on the environment. Here are just a few:

● Eating local produce when it is in season allows it to grow naturally, in a supportive environment that creates healthy, tasty food. It is cost-effective as well, because better growing conditions result in an increased supply and there is a lower cost as it's only transported a short distance. This is also known as sustainable living — using what is naturally produced and available locally.

● Taste, taste, taste — seasonal food tastes better! Simple as that. Correct sunlight, water and nutritious compost assists in the food's optimal development. Tomatoes, berries, peas and stone fruits taste sweet, flavoursome and juicy. Other vegetables, especially greens such as silverbeet (Swiss chard), lettuce, broccoli and cabbage have a bright, vibrant colour and are packed with nutrients. They are crisp, crunchy and sweet. They don't look wilted or taste bitter because they have been sitting on a shelf for ages or have been grown at the wrong time.

If you are lucky enough have a fruit tree or vine growing in your garden, take full advantage of it. Learn about pickling and preserving so that when the fruit is in season you don't waste any. If you simply can't make any more preserves or jams, give the rest of the fruit to your local school, friends or neighbours. It is wonderful to walk past a house with a box of fruit or vegetables out the front and a sign that says 'Free! Take some and enjoy.'

Lastly, remember to...

Learn about our environment — it is crucial to preserve the most important natural resource we have. Sustainable living is good for our health and good for the planet. If we respect and replenish nature, it will nurture us in return.

CHOP

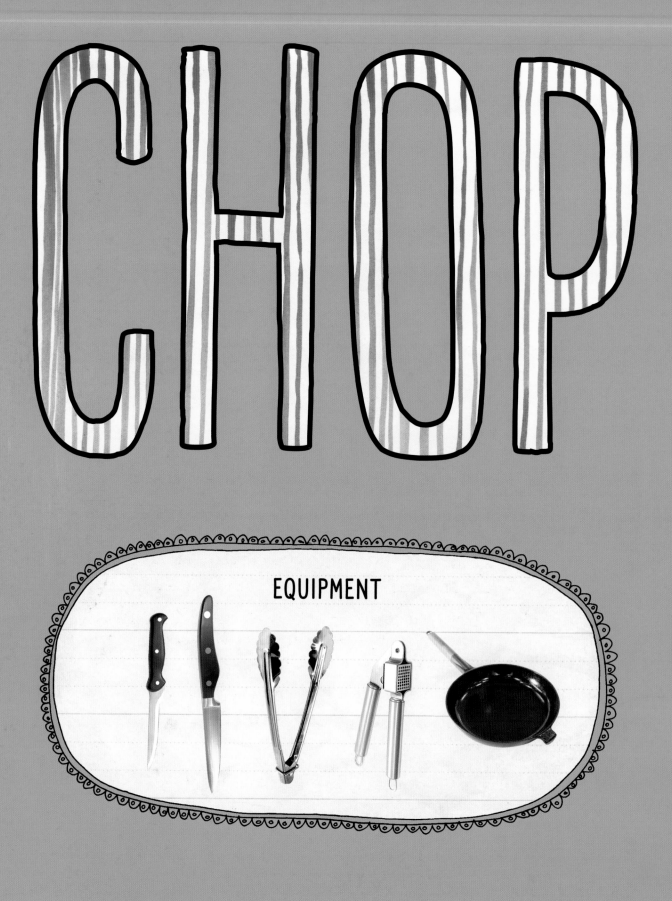

EQUIPMENT

Chopping is one of the first techniques I teach my students when cooking, probably because it's so important when preparing food. Most of the recipes in this chapter ask for a fine chop, which means chopping ingredients into very small cubes. Occasionally, you will be asked to slice ingredients, which means to chop them into thin strips. When chopping food into chunks or wedges, try to cut them into pieces of the same size. This is important because you want them to cook at the same rate. The more practice you have at chopping, the better you will become. Just take it slowly, focusing on your accuracy rather than speed, and always ask an adult for help if you need it.

MY SPAGHETTI BOLOGNESE

Everybody seems to have a version of spaghetti bolognese they call their own. This recipe has been adapted from my father's traditional spag bol and I'm sure that if I have children of my own, they will develop it even further!

Serves 6–8

2 tablespoons olive oil

1 brown onion, finely chopped

1 celery stalk, diced

4 garlic cloves, crushed

300 g (10½ oz) minced (ground) pork

300 g (10½ oz) minced (ground) veal

500 g (1 lb 2 oz) premium minced (ground) beef

250 ml (9 fl oz/1 cup) red wine (see helpful hint)

2 carrots, peeled and grated

2 x 400 g (14 oz) tins chopped tomatoes

700 ml (24 fl oz) tomato passata (puréed tomatoes)

100 g (3½ oz) mild salami, diced

2 tablespoons tomato paste (concentrated purée)

½ teaspoon dried chilli flakes (optional)

1 teaspoon dried oregano

1 teaspoon mixed dried herbs

1 tablespoon sugar

1 tablespoon balsamic vinegar

⅓ cup basil leaves, torn

spaghetti and freshly grated parmesan cheese, to serve

1 Prepare all the vegetables before you start cooking. Heat the oil in a large heavy-based saucepan over medium heat. Add the onion and celery and cook, stirring occasionally, for 5–6 minutes or until softened. Add the garlic and cook, stirring, for 1 minute more.

2 Increase the heat to high, add all the minced meat and cook until lightly browned, breaking up any lumps with a wooden spoon. Add the wine and cook, stirring occasionally, until it evaporates by at least half.

3 Stir in the carrots, tomatoes and passata, then the salami and tomato paste. Reduce the heat to low and simmer, uncovered, for 15 minutes.

4 Stir in the chilli flakes, dried herbs, sugar and vinegar. Season with salt and pepper, to taste. Simmer for a further 15 minutes or until the sauce is rich and thick. Add the basil and remove from the heat.

5 Serve your masterpiece spooned over spaghetti, with plenty of parmesan cheese sprinkled on top.

HELPFUL HINT
You can replace
the wine with the
same quantity of beef
stock or water
if you prefer.

VEGETABLE SKEWERS

WITH HALOUMI AND PARSLEY SAUCE

Haloumi is a Greek cheese that is traditionally made from sheep's or goat's milk. It has a salty taste and is great for frying and grilling because it holds its shape well. It is available from most supermarkets, greengrocers and delicatessens.

Makes 12

12 small metal or wooden skewers
2 red onions
2 red capsicums (peppers)
250 g (9 oz) haloumi cheese
3 zucchini (courgettes)
2 tablespoons olive oil,
  plus extra, to brush
1 tablespoon finely chopped
  rosemary

PARSLEY SAUCE

1 cup parsley leaves,
  finely chopped
80 ml (2½ fl oz/⅓ cup) olive oil
1 garlic clove, crushed
zest and juice of 1 lemon

1 If using wooden skewers, soak them in cold water for 20 minutes to prevent them burning during cooking.

2 Cut the onions, capsicums and haloumi into square, evenly sized pieces, about 2 x 2 cm (¾ x ¾ inch). Cut the zucchini into thick rounds. Thread the vegetables and haloumi onto the skewers. Combine the oil and rosemary in a small dish and brush over the vegetables to lightly coat.

3 To make the parsley sauce, combine the parsley, oil, garlic, lemon zest and juice in a bowl. Season with a good pinch of salt and some pepper and stir well.

4 Preheat a barbecue or chargrill pan to medium–high and then brush with the extra oil. Ask an adult for help if you need to. Grill the skewers for 2 minutes each side or until the vegetables and cheese are lightly charred and tender.

5 Serve the warm vegetable skewers with a drizzle of the parsley sauce.

TABOULEH

Tabouleh is a lovely Lebanese salad made with parsley and burghul, which is cracked wheat. It tastes best when the flavours have had time to develop, so once it's made cover it with plastic wrap and refrigerate for a few hours or overnight. Sumac is a popular Lebanese spice with a zesty lemon flavour, available from major supermarkets.

Serves 6

175 g (6 oz/1 cup) burghul (bulgar)

4 cups flat-leaf (Italian) parsley leaves, finely chopped

½ cup mint leaves, coarsely chopped

4 spring onions (scallions), trimmed, thinly sliced

10 cherry tomatoes, halved

1 Lebanese (short) cucumber, trimmed, diced

1 teaspoon sumac

80 ml (2½ fl oz/⅓ cup) lemon juice

80 ml (2½ fl oz/⅓ cup) olive oil

1 Put the burghul in a sieve and rinse under running water until the water runs clear. Transfer to a large heatproof bowl, cover with boiling water and set aside for 5–10 minutes or until just softened.

2 Meanwhile, put the herbs, spring onions, tomatoes and cucumber in a large bowl. Drain the burghul, pressing out as much excess water as possible.

3 Add the burghul to the salad, along with the sumac, lemon juice, oil, a good pinch of salt and some freshly ground black pepper. Toss to combine.

HELPFUL HINT
Basil is a very delicate herb that can bruise easily, so it's best to use the leaves whole or tear them gently with your fingers.

SUMMER PASTA SALAD

This fresh, colourful and flavour-packed pasta salad would be great to serve at a barbecue or party. Pick tomatoes that taste super-sweet and basil that smells very fragrant for the best results. We used a mixture of red, yellow and orange tomatoes.

Serves 6

500 g (1 lb 2 oz) fusilli pasta
1 cup basil leaves
250 g (9 oz) cherry tomatoes, halved
4 spring onions (scallions), trimmed, thinly sliced
6 slices prosciutto, cut into thin strips
200 g (7 oz) fresh ricotta cheese

DRESSING

1 garlic clove, crushed
½ teaspoon dijon mustard
60 ml (2 fl oz/¼ cup) balsamic vinegar
60 ml (2 fl oz/¼ cup) olive oil
1 teaspoon sugar

1 Bring a large saucepan of water to the boil, then add a large pinch of salt. Cook the pasta according to the packet instructions or until *al dente* (this means it has a little resistance when you bite into it), about 7–9 minutes. Drain well.

2 Meanwhile, combine the basil, tomatoes and spring onions in a large mixing bowl. Heat a small non-stick frying pan over medium heat and cook the prosciutto, stirring occasionally, for 2–3 minutes, until slightly crisp. Set aside to cool.

3 To make the dressing, put the garlic, mustard, vinegar, oil, sugar, a good pinch of salt and some freshly ground black pepper in a small bowl and whisk until combined.

4 Put the drained pasta, prosciutto and tomato mixture in a large serving bowl. Crumble over the ricotta and pour over the dressing. Gently toss to combine, and serve.

POTATO BAKE WITH SWEET LEEKS AND THYME

This is comfort food at its best. It makes a lovely side dish for roasted meats or you can serve it on its own with a green salad or a side dish, such as green beans. I have used gruyère cheese, which has a nutty flavour, but you could substitute cheddar cheese.

Serves 6

2 tablespoons unsalted butter
1 large leek, white part only,
   thinly sliced
1 tablespoon finely chopped thyme
5 large (about 150 g/5½ oz each)
   all-purpose potatoes, peeled
125 ml (4 fl oz/½ cup) milk
125 ml (4 fl oz/½ cup) thin
   (pouring/whipping) cream
100 g (3½ oz/1 cup) grated
   gruyère cheese

1 Preheat the oven to 210°C (415°F/Gas 6–7). Lightly grease a 1.5 litre (52 fl oz/6 cup) ovenproof baking dish. Melt the butter in a large frying pan over medium heat. Add the leek, a good pinch of salt and some pepper and cook, stirring occasionally, for 6–7 minutes or until soft. Remove from the heat and stir in the thyme.

2 Cut the potatoes in half, then place, cut side down, on a chopping board and slice thinly (see page 7). You might like to ask an adult for help.

half a potato!

3 Arrange enough potato slices in the greased dish, overlapping slightly, to cover the base. Sprinkle with some of the leek mixture. Continue layering the potato, sprinkling with the leek mixture after each layer. You should end up with 2–3 layers of potato. Whisk the milk and cream together in a jug, then pour evenly over the potatoes. Sprinkle with the cheese.

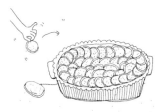

4 Cover the dish with foil and bake for 35–40 minutes. Carefully remove the foil and bake for 15–20 minutes or until the cheese is golden and potato is tender. You can insert a skewer into the potato to see if it's ready. Remove and set aside for 5 minutes to cool slightly before serving.

HELPFUL HINT

When moving dishes in and out of a hot oven, always wear a protective oven mitt and ask an adult to help you as the dish may be heavy, as well as very hot!

NEW WAVE COLESLAW

Serves 6

600 g (1 lb 5 oz/½ small) red
　cabbage, trimmed, outer
　leaves removed
2 carrots, peeled and grated
1 red onion, thinly sliced
40 g (1½ oz/¼ cup) currants
¼ cup flat-leaf (Italian) parsley
　leaves, coarsely chopped
¼ cup mint leaves, coarsely
　chopped
1 red capsicum (pepper)

DRESSING

250 ml (9 fl oz/1 cup)
　Greek-style yoghurt
juice of 1 lemon
2 teaspoons red wine vinegar

1 Wash and finely shred the cabbage. This means slicing
the cabbage as thinly as you can with a knife or using
a food processor with the fine slice attachment. You might
like to ask an adult for help.

2 Put the cabbage in a large mixing bowl and add the
carrots, onion, currants, parsley and mint. Cut the capsicum
in half from top to bottom and remove the seeds, stem and
white membrane. Cut the capsicum into thin strips and add
to the bowl.

3 To make the dressing, put the yoghurt, lemon juice,
vinegar, a good pinch of salt and some pepper in a small
bowl. Whisk until well combined, then spoon over the salad.
Toss the salad to coat in the dressing — I like to use my
hands for this. Serve.

THAI-STYLE CHICKEN BURGERS

WITH SWEET CHILLI SAUCE

Everybody loves a good burger, and making your own at home is a healthier option than buying takeaway. You can vary the toppings to use your favourite ingredients or whatever is growing in your garden, such as lettuce or tomatoes.

Serves 4

400 g (14 oz) minced (ground)
    skinless chicken thigh fillets
    (see helpful hints)
15 g (½ oz/¼ cup) fresh white
    breadcrumbs
1 small onion, finely chopped
1 garlic clove, crushed
2 tablespoons sweet chilli sauce,
    plus extra, to serve
1 free-range egg white,
    lightly whisked
¼ cup Thai basil leaves (see helpful
    hints), coarsely chopped
finely grated zest of 1 lime
1 tablespoon canola oil
4 burger buns, lightly toasted
new wave coleslaw (see page 39)
    or salad toppings, to serve

1 To make the chicken patties, combine the minced chicken, breadcrumbs, onion, garlic, sweet chilli sauce, egg white, basil and lime zest in a large mixing bowl. Season with a pinch of salt and some pepper. Divide the mixture into 4 equal portions, roll each into a large ball and flatten slightly to make 4 thick hamburger patties.

2 Heat the canola oil in a large non-stick frying pan over medium–high heat. Cook the patties for 4–5 minutes each side or until golden and cooked through.

3 To assemble the burgers, put some coleslaw or salad on the base of each bun. Top with a chicken patty, drizzle with extra sweet chilli sauce and cover with the top of the bun.

HELPFUL HINTS

Chicken thighs are relatively fatty so they make lovely juicy patties. You can ask your butcher to mince (grind) them for you.

● ● ●

Thai basil has a purple stem and flower, and is available from supermarkets and Asian grocers. You can substitute regular basil.

ASIAN COLD NOODLE SALAD

This salad is a favourite of mine. It has lots of texture thanks to the crunchy Asian fried noodles, which are available from supermarkets in the Asian ingredient section. The tangy Asian-style dressing can also be served with meats and fish.

Serves 4–6

100 g (3½ oz) baby spinach
  leaves, washed
1 Lebanese (short) cucumber,
  trimmed and sliced
2 spring onions (scallions),
  ends trimmed, thinly sliced
50 g (1¾ oz) snow pea
  (mangetout) sprouts
¼ cup mint leaves
100 g (3½ oz) young sugar snap
  peas, trimmed
50 g (1¾ oz) Asian fried noodles

NUOC MAM CHAM DRESSING

60 ml (2 fl oz/¼ cup) fish sauce
60 ml (2 fl oz/¼ cup) rice vinegar
2 tablespoons caster
  (superfine) sugar
125 ml (4 fl oz/½ cup) water
2 garlic cloves, crushed
1 long red chilli, seeded and
  thinly sliced (see helpful hint)
2 tablespoons lime juice

1 Put the spinach leaves, cucumber, spring onions and snow pea sprouts in a large salad bowl. Top with the mint, sugar snap peas, then noodles.

2 To make the nuoc mam cham dressing, put the fish sauce, rice vinegar, sugar and water in a saucepan over medium heat. Cook, stirring to dissolve the sugar, until just below boiling point (small bubbles will start to form around the edge of the pan). Set aside to cool.

3 Add the garlic, chilli and lime juice to the dressing and stir well. Pour 2–3 tablespoons of the dressing over the salad. (The remaining dressing will keep, in a sealed container in the refrigerator, for up to 3 days.)

HELPFUL HINT
Always wear disposable or rubber gloves when handling chillies. There are many varieties of chilli and each has a different strength of heat. Large red chillies available from supermarkets are mild. The hottest part of a chilli is the seeds and membrane attached to them, so remove these if you want less heat.

THE BEST EVER SCRAMBLED EGGS

WITH CROQUE MONSIEUR

If you want to treat Mum and Dad to breakfast in bed, serve them this. It is very simple to make and sure to impress. The key to light and fluffy scrambled eggs is to not overcook them. They will continue to cook even when you've turned the heat off, so remove them from the heat when they're still a little runny.

Serves 2

4 free-range eggs
1½ tablespoons milk
1 tablespoon crème fraîche
20 g (¾ oz) butter
flat-leaf (Italian) parsley leaves,
   to garnish

CROQUE MONSIEUR

4 slices ciabatta bread
2 teaspoons dijon mustard
80 g (2¾ oz) shaved leg ham
60 g (2¼ oz) gruyère cheese, sliced
2 teaspoons butter

1. Put the eggs, milk and crème fraîche in a large mixing bowl and whisk to combine.

2. To make the croque monsieur, put 2 ciabatta slices on a chopping board and spread with the mustard. Top with the ham and cheese. Cover with the remaining ciabatta slices. Spread the butter over the outside of each sandwich.

3. Heat a non-stick frying pan over medium–high heat. Cook the croque monsieurs for 1–2 minutes each side or until light golden and crisp. Set aside.

4. Melt the 20 g of butter over medium heat, then add the egg mixture. Cook for 20 seconds so it begins to set on the bottom, then stir gently, breaking the mixture up with a wooden spoon to create fluffy scrambled eggs. As soon as the eggs become thick and lumpy, turn off the heat. Season with a good pinch of salt and some pepper.

5. Serve the warm croque monsieur with scrambled eggs on the side and garnished with parsley leaves.

EASY PEAR AND LETTUCE SALAD

WITH CRUNCHY PARMESAN CROUTONS

Serves 4–6

½ loaf (about 300 g/10½ oz) day-old
    white bread, crusts removed
2 tablespoons olive oil
2 tablespoons finely grated
    parmesan cheese
1 butter lettuce, roots trimmed
1 Lebanese (short) cucumber,
    trimmed, thinly sliced
¼ cup roughly snipped chives
    (see helpful hints)
2 firm ripe pears, cored and thinly
    sliced (see helpful hints)
100 g (3½ oz) Danish feta cheese
1 quantity dijon dressing
    (see page 163)

1 Preheat the oven to 200°C (400°F/Gas 6). Tear the bread into bite-sized pieces and place in a large mixing bowl. Add the oil and parmesan and toss to coat. Place on a large baking tray and bake for 10 minutes or until light golden and crisp. Set aside to cool.

2 Wash the lettuce, separate the leaves and dry well. Place the leaves on a serving platter and top with the cucumber, chives and pears. Crumble over the feta and sprinkle with the baked croutons. Drizzle with the dijon dressing and serve immediately.

HELPFUL HINTS

To snip chives, hold the bunch in one hand and use kitchen scissors to snip off short lengths.

● ● ●

The best way to remove the core from the pears is to cut them into quarters, then lay each quarter on its flat side and run the knife from the top of the pear to the base. This will remove most of the core and any seeds.

CORN, ZUCCHINI AND FETA FRITTERS

These fritters are yummy eaten warm or cold for breakfast, lunch or dinner — any time, really! They also make a great addition to lunch boxes.

Makes 20

2½ tablespoons milk

1 free-range egg

1 large corn cob, kernels removed (see helpful hint)

1 medium zucchini (courgette), grated, squeezed of excess moisture

150 g (5½ oz) Greek feta cheese, crumbled

1 spring onion (scallion), ends trimmed, thinly sliced

60 g (2¼ oz) fresh ricotta cheese

120 g (4¼ oz) tin creamed corn

2 tablespoons snipped chives

2 tablespoons chopped flat-leaf (Italian) parsley

50 g (1¾ oz/⅓ cup) plain (all-purpose) flour

25 g (1 oz) butter

1 Whisk the milk and egg together in a small mixing bowl.

2 Combine the corn, zucchini, feta, spring onion, ricotta, creamed corn, chives and parsley in a separate bowl. Add the flour and season with a good pinch of salt and some pepper.

3 Add the egg mixture to the vegetables and stir until well combined.

4 Heat 2 teaspoons of the butter in a large non-stick frying pan over medium heat. Cooking 3–4 fritters at a time, spoon 1 tablespoon of the mixture into the pan for each fritter and use the back of the spoon to flatten slightly. Fry the fritters for 2–3 minutes each side or until golden brown. Transfer to a plate lined with paper towel while you cook the remaining fritters. Add a little extra butter to the pan if the fritters begin to stick during cooking.

HELPFUL HINT
To remove the corn kernels, hold the cob upright and use a sharp knife to slice off the kernels from the lower half. Turn the cob upside down and slice off the remaining kernels.

TUSCAN MEATBALLS

This recipe brings back fond childhood memories of pasta, pasta, pasta! It's all I wanted to eat at one stage and I still crave it now after a busy day. For this recipe, I like to use orecchiette pasta, which is shaped like a little ear.

Serves 4–6

60 ml (2 fl oz/¼ cup) olive oil

1 red onion, finely chopped

2 garlic cloves, crushed

400 g (14 oz) minced (ground) pork

400 g minced (ground) veal or beef

2 tablespoons flat-leaf (Italian) parsley leaves, chopped

1 tablespoon thyme leaves, chopped

60 g (2¼ oz/1 cup, lightly packed) fresh breadcrumbs

25 g (1 oz/¼ cup) finely grated parmesan cheese, plus extra, to serve

2 tablespoons tomato sauce (ketchup)

1 free-range egg, lightly whisked

500 g (1 lb 2 oz) orecchiette

8 baby bocconcini (fresh baby mozzarella cheese), halved

1 Heat 1½ tablespoons of the oil in a small frying pan over medium heat. Cook the onion, stirring often, for 3–4 minutes or until softened. Add the garlic and cook, stirring, for 1 minute. Transfer to a large bowl.

2 Add all the minced meat, the parsley, thyme, breadcrumbs, parmesan, tomato sauce, egg, a good pinch of salt and some pepper and use clean hands to mix the ingredients until combined. Place a bowl of water nearby to dip your fingers in (this will stop the mixture sticking to them). Roll tablespoons of the mixture into small balls and place on a tray.

tomato sauce

3 Heat the remaining 1½ tablespoons of oil in a large deep frying pan over medium–high heat. Cook the meatballs, in batches, for 2 minutes each side or until browned all over. Transfer to a plate and set aside. Clean the frying pan.

clean hands

TA–DAH!

SAUCE

1 tablespoon olive oil

1 garlic clove, crushed

2 x 400 g (14 oz) tins whole
    tomatoes

125 ml (4 fl oz/½ cup) chicken stock

1½ tablespoons balsamic vinegar

1 teaspoon sugar

¼ cup basil leaves, plus extra,
    to serve

4 To make the sauce, heat the oil in the frying pan and cook the garlic over medium heat, stirring often, for 30 seconds. Add the tomatoes and stock and bring to a simmer, then reduce the heat to low and cook, stirring occasionally with a wooden spoon to break up the tomatoes, for 10–15 minutes or until slightly thickened.

5 Meanwhile, bring a large saucepan of water to the boil, then add a large pinch of salt. Cook the pasta according to packet instructions or until *al dente* (it has a little resistance when you bite it). Drain well.

6 Add the vinegar, sugar and meatballs to the sauce and stir to combine. Taste and adjust the seasoning if needed and simmer for 2 minutes. Stir in the basil. Put the pasta in a large serving bowl, add the meatball sauce and scatter with the bocconcini. Stir gently to combine, top with extra basil and parmesan, and serve immediately.

WATERMELON, FETA AND MINT SALAD

WITH CITRUS DRESSING

Serves 4–6

½ small seedless watermelon
(about 2 kg/4 lb 8 oz),
rind removed
½ cup mint leaves
200 g (7 oz) Greek feta cheese

CITRUS DRESSING

juice of 1 orange
2 tablespoons olive oil

1 Cut the watermelon into bite-sized pieces, about 3 x 3 cm (1¼ x 1¼ inches). Arrange on a large plate and scatter with the mint. Crumble over the feta.

2 To make the citrus dressing, combine the orange juice and oil, and season with salt and pepper. Drizzle over the salad just before serving.

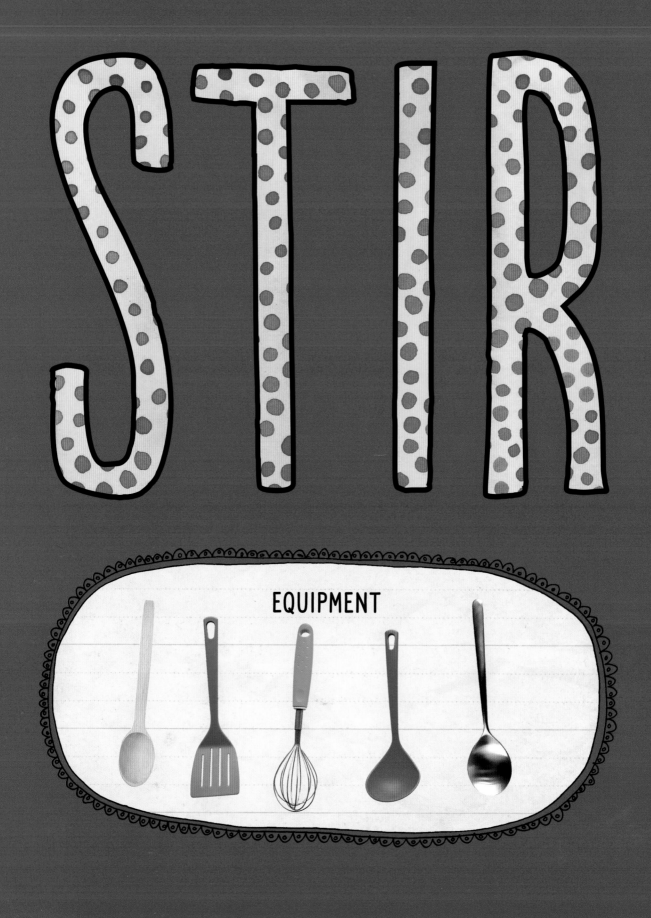

STIR

EQUIPMENT

There is something calming and satisfying about stirring an aromatic dish you have prepared from scratch. Delicious smells waft up from the pan as the spoon gently goes around, making your mouth water. I also find the act of stirring very informative. It can tell me whether a dish is finished or if it needs more time and attention, and whether its consistency is correct. You will find stirring soon becomes a skill that you can rely on. You will need the help of certain kitchen equipment (see opposite) — keep these utensils close at hand for this chapter, as they will become extensions of your arm.

RISOTTO OF SPRING PEAS, LEMON AND MASCARPONE

A risotto is actually quite simple to make and there are lots of flavour combinations you can try, such as chicken and mushroom, roasted tomato and chorizo, or roasted pumpkin, spinach and feta cheese. This recipe features mascarpone, an Italian cream cheese that can be used in both sweet and savoury dishes. It works beautifully in risotto, giving it a velvety, creamy finish.

Serves 4–6

1.25 litres (44 fl oz/5 cups)
   chicken stock
40 g (1½ oz) butter
1 tablespoon olive oil
1 small brown onion,
   finely chopped
1 celery stalk, finely chopped
2 garlic cloves, crushed
550 g (1 lb 4 oz/2½ cups)
   arborio rice
finely grated zest of 1 lemon
155 g (5½ oz/1 cup) shelled
   fresh spring peas
   (see helpful hints)
50 g (1¾ oz/½ cup) finely
   grated parmesan cheese,
   plus extra, to serve
1 heaped tablespoon
   mascarpone cheese

1 Bring the stock to the boil in a medium saucepan over high heat. Reduce the heat to very low and keep at a gentle simmer (small bubbles will rise slowly to the surface).

2 Heat the butter and oil in a large heavy-based saucepan over medium heat. Cook the onion and celery, stirring, for 2–3 minutes or until softened. Add the garlic and cook, stirring, for 1 minute. Add the rice and stir for about 2 minutes, until the grains are well coated with the butter and look glassy. This is an important step as it softens the outer layer of the rice.

3 Add the stock a ladleful at a time, stirring until almost all the stock has evaporated before adding each ladleful. Try to keep the risotto moist at all times.

4 When you have added all the stock and the rice is tender and creamy (this will take about 20 minutes), add the lemon zest, peas and parmesan. Season with salt and pepper and stir well. Remove from the heat and add the mascarpone, then cover and set aside for 2 minutes. Give the risotto a final stir before serving with extra parmesan cheese.

JAMBALAYA

This unique dish is a mixture of African, Spanish and American influences. It has lots of flavourings and spices, which make it an exciting and hearty rice meal that will warm you up beautifully during the cool winter months.

Serves 4–6

2 red capsicums (peppers)

1 tablespoon sweet paprika

pinch of cayenne pepper

1 teaspoon salt

1 teaspoon dried oregano

2 tablespoons olive oil

2 medium onions, finely chopped

3 celery stalks, trimmed,
   finely chopped

2 garlic cloves, crushed

2 tablespoons tomato paste
   (concentrated purée)

120 g (4¼ oz) chorizo sausage,
   sliced

200 g (7 oz) skinless chicken
   thigh fillets, diced

1 litre (35 fl oz/4 cups) chicken
   stock

400 g (14 oz/2 cups) white
   long-grain rice

400 g (14 oz) tin chopped tomatoes

1 bay leaf

2 tablespoons flat-leaf (Italian)
   parsley leaves, coarsely chopped,
   to garnish

1 Cut the capsicums in half from the top to the bottom, remove the seeds and white membrane and then finely chop the flesh. Combine the paprika, cayenne pepper, salt and oregano in a small bowl. Set aside.

2 Heat the oil in a large heavy-based saucepan over high heat. Cook the onions, celery and capsicums, stirring occasionally, for 2–3 minutes or until softened slightly. Add the garlic and cook, stirring, for 1 minute more. Add the spice mixture and stir to coat. Add the tomato paste, chorizo and chicken and cook, stirring constantly, for 2 minutes or until the chorizo starts to brown slightly around the edges.

3 Add the stock, rice, tomatoes and bay leaf to the pan and stir to combine. Bring to a simmer (small bubbles will rise slowly to the surface), then reduce the heat to low and simmer for 20–25 minutes or until the rice is tender and has absorbed most of the liquid, but the dish is still a little moist. Taste and season with salt and pepper, if needed. Garnish with parsley just before serving.

SEMOLINA GNOCCHI

WITH TOMATO SUGO

My students love making this dish, and it is a wonderful family meal. Gnocchi can be based on potatoes, ricotta or semolina, as it is here. Semolina, available from supermarkets, is made by grinding durum wheat and can be fine or coarse.

Serves 4

GNOCCHI

600 ml (21 fl oz) milk

1 bay leaf

2 rosemary sprigs

150 g (5½ oz) fine semolina

1 egg yolk

60 g (2¼ oz) finely grated
   parmesan cheese

30 g (1 oz) unsalted butter, melted

100 g (3½ oz) buffalo mozzarella
   cheese, sliced

8 basil leaves

TOMATO SUGO

1 tablespoon olive oil

½ red onion, finely chopped

1 garlic clove, crushed

400 g (14 oz) tin chopped tomatoes

60 ml (2 fl oz/¼ cup) water

1 teaspoon light brown sugar

1 tablespoon thyme leaves

1 To make the gnocchi, put the milk, bay leaf and rosemary in a saucepan over low heat and bring to a gentle simmer (small bubbles will rise slowly to the surface). Turn off the heat and set aside for 10 minutes.

2 Remove the herbs and bring the milk to the boil over low heat. Gradually sprinkle in the semolina, whisking constantly. Season with a good pinch of salt. Use a wooden spoon to continue stirring until the mixture starts to come away from the side of the pan.

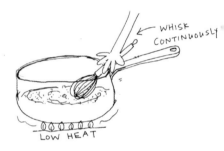

3 Remove from the heat and stir in the egg yolk, parmesan and butter until combined. Tip onto a slightly damp work surface and shape into 2 logs, each about 35 cm (14 inches) long. Allow to cool slightly.

4 Preheat the oven to 180°C (350°F/Gas 4). Grease an 18 x 28 cm (7 x 11¼ inch) ovenproof dish or four individual dishes with butter. Cut the semolina logs into 1.5 cm (⅝ inch) pieces and place in a single layer in the greased dish or dishes.

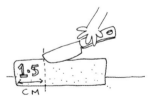

5 To make the tomato sugo, heat the oil in a medium frying pan over medium heat. Cook the onion, stirring occasionally, for 5 minutes or until softened. Add the garlic and cook, stirring, for 1 minute. Add the tomatoes and water, reduce the heat to low and simmer gently, stirring occasionally, for 12–15 minutes or until thickened. Add the sugar, thyme, a good pinch of salt and some pepper, stir well and simmer for a further 5 minutes. Pour over the gnocchi, then top with the mozzarella and basil. Bake for 20–25 minutes or until the cheese is golden brown. Serve.

HELPFUL HINT

When making soups it is important to chop the vegetables into evenly sized pieces so they cook at the same rate.

SPICED CARROT, CHICKPEA AND CORIANDER SOUP

Serves 4–6

25 g (1 oz) butter

1 tablespoon olive oil

1 onion, finely chopped

2 garlic cloves, crushed

1 large sweet potato, peeled, cut
into 4 cm (1½ inch) chunks

3 large carrots, peeled, cut into
4 cm (1½ inch) chunks

1 teaspoon ground cumin

1 teaspoon ground turmeric

1 teaspoon ground coriander

1 litre (35 fl oz/4 cups) chicken
stock

400 g (14 oz) tin chickpeas,
drained and rinsed

60 ml (2 fl oz/¼ cup) thickened
(whipping) cream

2 tablespoons chopped coriander
(cilantro) leaves

lemon wedges, to serve

1 Heat the butter and oil in a large deep saucepan over medium heat. Cook the onion, stirring occasionally, for 3–4 minutes or until softened. Add the garlic and cook, stirring, for 1 minute. Add the sweet potato and carrots and stir to coat in the onion mixture. Add the spices and cook, stirring, for 1 minute more.

2 Add the stock and bring to the boil, then reduce the heat to low and add the chickpeas. Cover the pan and simmer (small bubbles will rise slowly to the surface) gently for 20 minutes or until the vegetables are tender.

3 Remove the soup from the heat and set aside for 20 minutes to cool slightly (it is dangerous to blend soup while it is very hot). Blend the soup in batches using a stick blender or regular blender, until it is smooth.

4 Return the soup to a clean pan and reheat gently over medium heat. Season with a good pinch of salt and some pepper. Stir in the cream and serve sprinkled with the coriander and accompanied by lemon wedges.

BROCCOLI, LEEK AND TARRAGON TART

My shortcrust pastry works beautifully in this tart. However, if time is an issue, you can use a ready-made shortcrust shell instead.

Serves 6

1 quantity shortcrust pastry
  (see page 109)
450 g (1 lb) broccoli,
  cut into small florets
50 g (1¾ oz) butter
1 leek, white part only,
  thinly sliced
6 free-range eggs,
  lightly whisked
350 ml (12 fl oz) thickened
  (whipping) cream
100 g (3½ oz/1 cup) grated
  cheddar cheese
¼ cup tarragon leaves,
  coarsely chopped
mixed salad leaves, to serve

1 Preheat the oven to 210°C (415°F/Gas 6–7). Grease a round 26 cm (10½ inch) loose-based fluted tart (flan) tin with butter. Roll the pastry out between 2 sheets of non-stick baking paper until it is about 3 mm (1/8 inch) thick. Remove the top sheet of paper and gently flip the pastry over the tin. Remove the remaining paper and gently press the pastry into the tin, making sure it fills the edges. Use a small sharp knife to trim the excess pastry — I always trim pastry about 1 cm (½ inch) above the tin as it can shrink a little during cooking. Place the pastry-lined tin on a baking tray and refrigerate for 15 minutes.

2 Cover the pastry with non-stick baking paper and fill it with dried beans, uncooked rice or baking beads. Bake for 15 minutes, then remove the paper and weights and bake for a further 6–7 minutes, until it is pale and slightly crisp. The edges should be slightly golden. Set aside to cool. Reduce the oven temperature to 200°C (400°F/Gas 6).

3 Meanwhile, blanch the broccoli florets in a saucepan of boiling water for 3 minutes or until bright green and tender. Refresh under cold running water. Drain well.

4 Melt the butter in a frying pan over medium heat. Cook the leek, stirring occasionally, for 5–6 minutes, until soft. Set aside. Whisk the eggs, cream, cheese, tarragon and some salt and pepper in a mixing bowl until combined.

5 Scatter the leek over the pastry shell, followed by the broccoli. Carefully pour over the egg mixture. You might like to ask an adult to put it in the oven for you. Bake the tart for 30–35 minutes or until the filling is firm and slightly golden. Set aside for 5 minutes to cool slightly before cutting into slices. Serve with mixed salad leaves.

HELPFUL HINT

If your pastry cracks during blind baking, patch the holes with small pieces of leftover pastry or brush with a little whisked egg and bake for a few minutes more to seal.

MINI PORK AND SAGE PIES

I absolutely love making pies. It's fun to play around with different flavour combinations and I encourage you to have a go. Pies also freeze well — assemble them but don't cook, then wrap well and freeze. Bake, without thawing, for 20–25 minutes in a 220°C oven.

Serves 6

2 tablespoons olive oil

2 bacon rashers, rind removed, diced

2 garlic cloves, crushed

4 French shallots, finely chopped

1 celery stalk, diced

1 carrot, peeled and diced

500 g (1 lb 2 oz) minced (ground) pork

2 tablespoons plain (all-purpose) flour

2 tablespoons tomato paste (concentrated purée)

250 ml (9 fl oz/1 cup) veal or chicken stock

125 ml (4 fl oz/½ cup) water

¼ cup sage leaves, coarsely chopped

1 fresh bay leaf

1 tablespoon coarsely chopped thyme

1½ tablespoons thin (pouring/ whipping) cream

2 sheets frozen ready-made puff pastry, thawed

1 egg, lightly whisked

cooked green peas, to serve

1 Heat the oil in a large saucepan over medium heat. Cook the bacon, stirring occasionally, for 4–5 minutes or until light golden. Transfer to a plate and set aside.

2 Add the garlic, shallots, celery and carrot to the pan and cook, stirring often, for 3–4 minutes or until softened. Add the pork and cook, breaking it up with a wooden spoon, for 5 minutes or until browned. Return the bacon to the pan.

3 Add the flour and tomato paste and cook, stirring, for 1 minute. Add the stock, water, sage, bay leaf and thyme and simmer (small bubbles will rise slowly to the surface), uncovered, for 10 minutes or until thickened. Stir in the cream, season with salt and pepper and cook for 1 minute more. The mixture should be thick and moist. Remove the bay leaf and discard.

4 Preheat the oven to 220°C (425°F/Gas 7).

5 Divide the pork mixture among six 160 ml (5¼ fl oz/ ⅔ cup) ovenproof ramekins. Use a round 10 cm (4 inch) cutter to cut 6 circles from the pastry. (They need to be slightly larger than the ramekins.) Top each ramekin with a pastry circle and gently press the pastry down around the rims to seal. Brush the pastry with the egg and prick with a fork so the steam can be released during cooking. Bake the pies for 15–20 minutes or until puffed and golden. Set aside for 5 minutes to cool slightly before serving with peas.

LINGUINE

WITH ONION, CHORIZO AND OLIVES

Serves 4

500 g (1 lb 2 oz) fresh linguine
(see page 100) or 350 g (12 oz)
dried linguine
1 tablespoon olive oil
1 red onion, thinly sliced
1 chorizo sausage, thinly sliced
2 x 400 g (14 oz) tins whole
tomatoes
75 g (2¾ oz/½ cup) pitted
kalamata olives
1 tablespoon finely chopped
rosemary
1 long red chilli, seeded and
finely chopped (optional)
shaved or finely grated parmesan
cheese, to serve

1 Bring a large saucepan of water to the boil, then add a large pinch of salt. Cook the pasta, following the instructions on the packet or until *al dente* (this means it has a little resistance when you bite into it). Fresh pasta will only take 3–4 minutes. Drain well.

2 Heat the oil in a large frying pan over medium heat and cook the onion and chorizo, stirring, for 5–6 minutes or until the onion is soft and golden.

3 Add the tomatoes and olives to the pan and simmer (small bubbles will rise slowly to the surface), breaking up the tomatoes with a wooden spoon, for 12–13 minutes or until the sauce is thick.

4 Add the rosemary and chilli, if using, to the sauce and season with salt and pepper, to taste. Cook for a further 2 minutes. Add the pasta to the sauce and toss to coat. Serve topped with parmesan cheese.

HELPFUL HINT
Always wear disposable or rubber gloves when handling chillies, to avoid getting capsaicin (which is responsible for the heat) on your hands as you may rub your eyes or put them in your mouth afterwards.

MINI QUICHES

WITH ZUCCHINI CRUSTS

I use zucchini ribbons instead of a pastry crust for these delicious little quiches.

Makes 12

2–3 large zucchini (courgettes)

150 g (5½ oz) bacon, rind removed, finely chopped

6 free-range eggs

125 ml (4 fl oz/½ cup) thickened (whipping) cream

¼ teaspoon freshly grated nutmeg (see helpful hint)

100 g (3½ oz) baby spinach leaves, finely chopped

1 Preheat the oven to 200°C (400°F/ Gas 6). Use a vegetable peeler to peel each zucchini into long thin ribbons, stopping when you reach the seeds in the centre and turning it over to peel more ribbons from the other side — you will need 24 ribbons.

you'll need 24 ribbons!

2 Heat a medium non-stick frying pan over medium heat and cook the bacon, stirring occasionally, for 3–5 minutes or until crisp around the edges. Transfer to a plate lined with paper towels to drain.

3 Put the eggs, cream and nutmeg in a large mixing bowl, season with salt and pepper and whisk lightly to combine. Stir in the spinach leaves and bacon.

4 Lightly grease a 12-hole 80 ml (2½ fl oz/⅓ cup) muffin tin. Cut twelve 14 cm (5½ inch) squares of non-stick baking paper and use to line each muffin hole, with the paper rising above the sides. Curl 2 zucchini ribbons inside each lined muffin hole to form neat rings. Divide the egg mixture among the muffin holes.

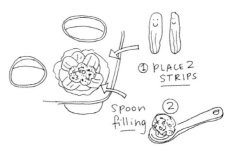

① PLACE 2 STRIPS

Spoon filling ②

5 Bake the quiches for 15–20 minutes or until the filling is set and golden. Remove from the oven and set aside for a few minutes, until cool enough to handle. Use the paper to lift the quiches out of the tin, then carefully peel the paper away. Serve the quiches warm or keep in an airtight container in the refrigerator for up to 2 days and bring to room temperature to serve.

HELPFUL HINT

To grate nutmeg, you can use tiny graters designed especially for this purpose, available from kitchenware stores, a Microplane or the fine side of a regular grater. If you can't find whole nutmeg, use ground nutmeg instead.

ROLL

EQUIPMENT

Our hands will always be our most useful and practical tools when cooking. This is the traditional way of cooking, before machines and gadgets did all the work. Touching food is an excellent way to judge its texture and gives you a greater sense of connection to it. This chapter contains some of my favourite recipes, and my students have enjoyed making and eating them, too. In my experience, the act of rolling ingredients has to be one of the most enjoyable experiences when cooking. Tasks that may have appeared lengthy fly by with giggles about the perfect size to roll and lovely chit-chat. I know you will enjoy making the recipes in this chapter and hope they get your conversations rolling, too.

CRUNCHY THREE-CHEESE BALLS

Makes about 20

500 g (1 lb 2 oz) mozzarella cheese,
  coarsely grated
100 g (3½ oz) parmesan cheese,
  coarsely grated
300 g (10½ oz) fresh ricotta cheese
2 tablespoons chopped thyme
110 g (3¾ oz/¾ cup) plain
  (all-purpose) flour
2 free-range eggs, lightly whisked
75 g (2¾ oz/1½ cups) panko
  (Japanese) breadcrumbs
  (see helpful hints)
canola oil, for deep-frying

1 Put the cheeses and thyme in a large mixing bowl and use clean hands to mix until well combined. Season with a good pinch of salt and some pepper.

2 Roll 2 tablespoons of the cheese mixture into a ball and place on a large baking tray. Repeat with the remaining mixture. Set up a crumbing station with three shallow bowls — one with the flour, a second with the eggs and a third with the breadcrumbs. Toss a cheese ball in the flour to lightly coat, then dip in the egg, allowing the excess to drip off, and finally coat in the breadcrumbs. Repeat to coat the remaining balls.

3 Pour enough oil into a medium saucepan to come halfway up the side of the pan. Heat over low heat until the oil reaches 180°C (350°F) or a cube of bread dropped into the oil turns golden brown in 15 seconds (see helpful hints, and the safety tips for frying on page 11). Use a slotted spoon to carefully lower the balls, a few at a time, into the hot oil and fry for 2–3 minutes, turning once, or until golden and crisp. Use the slotted spoon to transfer to paper towels to drain while you cook the remaining balls. Serve warm.

HELPFUL HINTS

Panko breadcrumbs are available from supermarkets and delicatessens. You can use regular dried breadcrumbs instead.

● ● ●

Another way to test if the oil is hot enough is to stick the end of a wooden spoon in it. If the oil bubbles about the wood, it is ready.

FOCACCIA

WITH ROASTED CAPSICUM, OLIVES AND ROSEMARY

This focaccia is fun and easy to make. Top it with whatever you like, but don't go overboard or the topping will weigh down the focaccia while baking.

Serves 6

7 g (⅛ oz/2 teaspoons) dried yeast
375 ml (13 fl oz/1½ cups) lukewarm
   water
500 g (1 lb 2 oz/3⅓ cups) plain
   (all-purpose) flour
1 teaspoon salt
2 tablespoons extra virgin olive oil,
   plus extra, to grease
2 red capsicums (peppers), halved,
   seeds and membranes removed
75 g (2¾ oz/½ cup) pitted kalamata
   olives, sliced
2 teaspoons rosemary leaves
100 g (3½ oz) Greek feta cheese,
   crumbled
olive oil, to drizzle

1 Preheat the oven to 200°C (400°F/Gas 6).

2 Put the yeast in a small bowl, add the lukewarm water and stir to combine. Set aside for 5–10 minutes or until foamy (this means the yeast has activated).

3 Sift the flour into a large bowl and add the salt. Make a well (a small hole) in the centre of the flour. Add the oil and the yeast mixture and use a wooden spoon and then clean hands to mix until a soft, yet firm dough forms. Transfer the dough to a lightly floured work surface and knead until it is smooth, elastic and shiny (about 10 minutes). If you have a stand mixer with a dough hook attachment, you could use it to knead the dough.

4 Put the dough in a lightly oiled bowl, rub the top with oil, cover with plastic wrap and set aside to prove in a warm, draught-free place for 1 hour or until doubled in size.

5 Meanwhile, place the capsicums on a large baking tray, skin side up, and roast for 25 minutes or until slightly blistered. Transfer to an airtight

container for 5 minutes. This will sweat the capsicums and make the skin easy to remove. When they are cool enough to handle, peel away the skin and slice the flesh into thin strips. Reduce the oven temperature to 180°C (350°F/Gas 4).

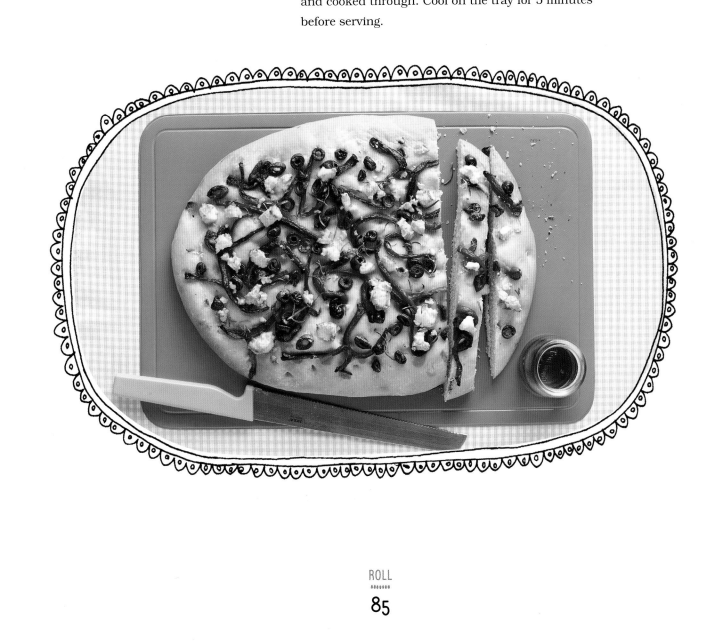

6 Lightly oil a 20 x 30 cm (8 x 12 inch) non-stick baking tray and place the dough in the centre. Lightly rub some oil on your fingers, then push the dough out to make a large oval shape of even thickness that extends to the length and width of the tray. Poke your fingers all over the surface to make indentations.

7 Scatter the capsicum strips, olives and rosemary over the focaccia, leaving a small border for the crust. Season with salt and pepper, sprinkle over the crumbled feta and drizzle with a little olive oil.

8 Bake the focaccia for 30–40 minutes or until golden and cooked through. Cool on the tray for 5 minutes before serving.

LENTIL AND COUSCOUS PATTIES

These patties are a great vegetarian snack or healthy dinner. Originally they were just lentil patties, but one day the mixture was a little wet so I added couscous and it worked a treat! I like to serve them with raita and a wedge of lemon on the side.

Makes 15

305 g (10¾ oz/1½ cups) dried
    red split lentils
750 ml (26 fl oz/3 cups) water
1 onion, finely chopped
2 cm (¾ inch) piece fresh ginger,
    peeled and grated
1 teaspoon salt
½ teaspoon ground cinnamon
pinch of ground cloves
1 fresh bay leaf (see helpful hint)
95 g (3¼ oz/½ cup) couscous
1 egg
1 tablespoon finely chopped mint
1 carrot, peeled and grated
60 g (2¼ oz/1 cup) panko (Japanese)
    breadcrumbs (see helpful hint,
    page 82)
125 ml (4 fl oz/½ cup) vegetable oil
raita (see page 138) and lemon
    wedges, to serve

1 Put the lentils in a medium saucepan with the water, onion, ginger, salt, spices and bay leaf. Bring to the boil over high heat, then reduce the heat to low and simmer, stirring occasionally, for 12–15 minutes or until the lentils are just tender. Remove from the heat and discard the bay leaf.

2 Put the warm lentil mixture in a large bowl, add the couscous and stir until just combined. Cover with plastic wrap and set aside for 5–10 minutes. The couscous will absorb any moisture and cook a little from the heat of the lentils. Add the egg, mint, carrot, salt and pepper and stir to combine. Transfer to a bowl, cover with plastic wrap and refrigerate for 1 hour or until firm.

3 Put the breadcrumbs in a shallow bowl. Shape 2 heaped tablespoons of the lentil mixture into a patty and toss in the breadcrumbs to coat. Place on a baking tray and repeat with the remaining lentil mixture to make 15 patties.

4 Heat the oil in a large frying pan over medium heat. Fry the patties, in batches, for 2–3 minutes each side or until light golden and crisp. Serve the patties with the raita and lemon wedges.

HELPFUL HINT
You can use a dried bay leaf, but fresh ones have more flavour.

GOZLEME

This recipe calls for Persian feta cheese, which is soft, rich and creamy as it is marinated in oil with herbs, spices and sometimes garlic. If you can't find it, use regular feta instead.

Serves 6

200 g (7 oz/¾ cup) Greek-style
  yoghurt
1 tablespoon olive oil
1 teaspoon sea salt
250 g (9 oz/1²/₃ cups) self-raising
  flour
lemon wedges, to serve

FILLING

1 tablespoon olive oil, plus extra,
  to brush
250 g (9 oz) minced (ground) lamb
1 garlic clove, crushed
1 teaspoon ground cumin
400 g (14 oz) tin chopped tomatoes
1 tablespoon honey
100 g (3½ oz) baby spinach,
  coarsely chopped
100 g (3½ oz) Persian feta cheese,
  crumbled

1 Put the yoghurt, oil and salt in a large mixing bowl and stir to combine. Gradually add the flour, folding it in with a spatula, until a stiff dough forms. Transfer the dough to a lightly floured work surface and knead until it is smooth and elastic, about 5 minutes. Place it in a lightly oiled bowl, cover with plastic wrap and set aside for 30 minutes to rest.

2 Meanwhile, to make the filling, heat the oil in a large frying pan over high heat. Cook the lamb, breaking it up with a wooden spoon, for 3–4 minutes or until browned. Add the garlic and cumin and cook, stirring, for 1 minute. Add the tomatoes and honey, season with salt and pepper, and simmer for 15 minutes or until thick. Remove from the heat and stir through the spinach leaves. Set aside to cool.

3 To make the gözleme, divide the dough into 6 equal portions and roll each into a ball. Working with one ball at a time, use a lightly floured rolling pin to roll out the dough on a lightly floured surface until it forms a circle, about 18 cm (7 inches) in diameter and 2 mm ($^1/_{16}$ inch) thick. Spread one-sixth of the filling over half the circle, then top with some crumbled feta. Fold the uncovered dough over to make a semi-circle, enclosing the filling. Pinch the edges to seal. Repeat to make the remaining gözleme. Brush both sides of each gözleme with oil.

4 Preheat a char-grill pan or barbecue plate on medium heat. Cook the gözleme, in batches if necessary, for 2–3 minutes each side or until they are lightly charred. Serve warm with lemon wedges.

PUMPKIN ARANCINI

WITH SAGE AND GOOEY MOZZARELLA

Makes about 20

150 g (5½ oz/1 cup) plain
  (all-purpose) flour
2 free-range eggs, lightly whisked
120 g (4¼ oz/2 cups) panko
  (Japanese) breadcrumbs
  (see helpful hint, page 82)
canola oil, for deep-frying

RISOTTO

300 g (10½ oz) peeled and seeded
  pumpkin, cut into 1 cm
  (½ inch) dice
8 sage leaves, coarsely chopped
2 tablespoons olive oil
1 litre (35 fl oz/4 cups) chicken
  stock
20 g (¾ oz) butter
1 white onion, finely chopped
1 garlic clove, crushed
440 g (15½ oz/2 cups) arborio rice
100 g (3½ oz/1 cup) finely grated
  parmesan cheese
125 g (4½ oz) mozzarella cheese,
  cut into 1 cm (½ inch) cubes

1 Preheat the oven to 200°C (400°F/Gas 6).

2 To make the risotto, put the pumpkin and sage on a large baking tray, drizzle with 1 tablespoon of the oil, season with salt and pepper and toss to combine. Roast for 20 minutes or until just tender. Set aside.

3 Meanwhile, bring the stock to the boil in a small saucepan. Reduce the heat to low and keep at a gentle simmer (small bubbles will rise slowly to the surface).

4 Heat the butter and remaining oil in a large saucepan over medium heat. Cook the onion, stirring occasionally, for 3–4 minutes or until softened. Add the garlic and cook, stirring, for 1 minute. Add the rice and stir for about 2 minutes, until the grains are well coated with the butter and look glassy. Add the stock a ladleful at a time, stirring until almost all the stock has evaporated before adding each ladleful. Try to keep the risotto moist at all times.

5 When you have added all the stock and the rice is tender and creamy (about 20 minutes), add the pumpkin and sage, the parmesan, a pinch of salt and some pepper. Stir gently to combine, then remove from the heat and set aside until cool enough to handle.

6 Set up a crumbing station with three shallow bowls — one with the flour, a second with the eggs and a third with the breadcrumbs.

7 Roll 2 tablespoons of risotto into a ball, push a cube of mozzarella into the middle and push the risotto over to cover it completely. Put on a tray and repeat with the remaining risotto and mozzarella cubes. Roll each ball in flour, then egg, allowing any excess to drip off, and coat in breadcrumbs.

Mozzarella!

8 Pour enough oil into a medium saucepan to come halfway up the side. Heat over low heat until the oil reaches 180°C (350°F) or a cube of bread dropped into the oil turns golden brown in 15 seconds. (See the safety tips for frying on page 11). Use a slotted spoon to lower the balls, a few at a time, into the oil and fry for 4 minutes, turning once, or until golden. Use the slotted spoon to transfer to paper towels to drain while you cook the remaining balls. Serve warm.

ROLL

A TALE OF TWO PIZZAS

Pizzas are a blank canvas for flavour so I encourage you to experiment. Here are two of my favourite toppings for inspiration (both make enough for 2 pizzas).

Serves 4–6

DOUGH

7 g (⅛ oz/2 teaspoons) dried yeast
1 teaspoon sugar
250 ml (9 fl oz/1 cup) lukewarm
  water
375 g (13 oz/2½ cups) plain
  (all-purpose) flour
1 teaspoon salt
1 tablespoon olive oil

PROSCIUTTO TOPPING

125 ml (4 fl oz/½ cup) tomato
  passata (puréed tomatoes)
5 slices prosciutto, torn
250 g (9 oz) buffalo mozzarella
  cheese, sliced
10 basil leaves

POTATO TOPPING

60 ml (2 fl oz/¼ cup) olive oil
2 medium waxy potatoes,
  thinly sliced
80 g (2¾ oz/¾ cup) finely grated
  pecorino cheese
1 tablespoon finely chopped
  rosemary

1 To make the dough, put the yeast in a small bowl, add the sugar and water and stir to combine. Set aside for 5–10 minutes or until foamy (this means the yeast has activated). Put the flour, salt and oil in a large bowl and make a well (a small hole) in the centre. Pour in the yeast mixture and use your fingertips to combine the ingredients until a dough starts to form. Turn out onto a lightly floured surface and knead for 5 minutes or until smooth and elastic. Place in a lightly oiled bowl, rub the top with oil, cover with a tea towel (dish towel) and set aside to prove in a warm, draught-free place for 30 minutes, until doubled in size.

2 Preheat the oven to 220°C (425°F/Gas 7).

3 Punch the dough down once with your fist, then divide it into 4 equal portions and roll each portion into a ball. Use a lightly floured rolling pin to roll out one ball at a time on a lightly floured surface to your desired thickness. I like my pizza bases thin, about 20 cm (8 inches) in diameter. Place on lightly oiled baking trays.

4 For the prosciutto topping, brush 2 bases with passata, leaving a border, then top with prosciutto and mozzarella. For the potato topping, brush 2 pizza bases with some of the oil and top with the potato slices, pecorino and rosemary, leaving a border. Season the potatoes with a good pinch of sea salt and drizzle with the remaining oil.

5 Bake the pizzas for 10–15 minutes or until golden around the edges and the cheese has melted and/or the potato is tender. Top the prosciutto pizza with basil. Serve.

LITTLE CRUMBED FISHCAKES

Makes 12–14

400 g (14 oz) potatoes (such as
   desiree), cut into chunks
20 g (¾ oz) butter
1 garlic clove, crushed
300 g (10½ oz) flathead fillets
   (or other firm white-fleshed
   fish fillets)
3 spring onions (scallions),
   ends trimmed, sliced
1 tablespoon finely chopped parsley
150 g (5½ oz/1 cup) plain
   (all-purpose) flour
2 free-range eggs, lightly whisked
90 g (3¼ oz/1½ cups) panko
   (Japanese) breadcrumbs
   (see helpful hint, page 82)
2 tablespoons vegetable oil
good-quality ready-made aïoli and
   lemon wedges, to serve

1 Cook the potatoes in a large saucepan of lightly salted boiling water for 8–10 minutes or until tender. Drain well and set aside.

2 Melt the butter in a medium frying pan over medium–high heat. Cook the garlic, stirring, for 20 seconds. Add the fish fillets and cook for 2–3 minutes, then turn and cook for 1 minute more. Remove from the heat.

3 Put the potatoes in a large mixing bowl and use a potato masher to mash. Add the spring onions, parsley, a good pinch of salt and some pepper. Flake (break up with a fork) the fish fillets and add to the bowl. Stir until just combined, then shape the mixture into 12 round patties of similar size. Place on a plate, covered, in the refrigerator for 15–20 minutes to firm.

4 Set up a crumbing station with three shallow bowls — one with the flour, a second with the eggs and a third with the breadcrumbs. Dust the patties in the flour to lightly coat, then dip in the eggs, allowing the excess to drip off, and finally coat in the breadcrumbs. Repeat with the remaining patties.

5 Heat the oil in a large frying pan over medium heat. Cook the fishcakes, in batches, for 1–2 minutes each side or until golden. Serve immediately with aïoli and lemon wedges.

HELPFUL HINT

Overcooking fishcakes is a common mistake. Remember that the inside is already cooked, so you just want to crisp and colour them.

MIX

EQUIPMENT

This chapter is all about the joys of mixing — cakes, biscuits, tarts, puddings and even the odd savoury treat, too. These days, there are many helpful kitchen tools that make mixing easier, such as electric stand mixers and hand-held beaters. However, I still take pleasure from the good old-fashioned way of mixing, using a large wooden spoon (and licking it clean at the end). Working on your mixing technique will also help you improve your licking technique, it's a win-win situation! On a more serious note, it is important to beat, cream, whisk, process, combine and fold ingredients with the appropriate equipment. My helpful hints will guide you along the way.

CRUNCHY CAULIFLOWER PAKORAS

These lightly spiced bites are great served as a starter before dinner or even as a snack. I like to serve them with raita for dipping. You could also use this batter for other vegetables such as broccoli or carrot.

Serves 4

300 g (10½ oz) cauliflower,
   trimmed, cut into florets
100 g (3½ oz) besan
   (chickpea flour)
½ teaspoon ground turmeric
½ teaspoon cumin seeds
½ teaspoon black mustard seeds
½ teaspoon ground coriander
150 ml (5 fl oz) chilled water,
   approximately
½ teaspoon baking powder
vegetable oil, for deep-frying
raita (see page 138), to serve

1 Cook the cauliflower in a large saucepan of boiling water for 2 minutes, then drain and put in a bowl of cold water. This technique is called blanching and involves cooking vegetables in boiling water for a short time, then refreshing them in cold water to stop the cooking process.

2 Combine the besan and spices in a large mixing bowl. Gradually stir in the water, adding enough to make a thick batter that coats the back of a wooden spoon. Whisk to remove any lumps. Whisk in the baking powder and season with salt and pepper. Add the cauliflower florets.

3 Pour enough oil into a medium saucepan to come halfway up the side of the pan. Heat over medium heat until the oil reaches 180°C (350°F) or a cube of bread dropped into the oil turns golden brown in 15 seconds. (See the safety tips for frying on page 11). Use a slotted spoon to lift 2 or 3 cauliflower florets out of the batter, letting any excess drain off. Carefully lower them into the hot oil to cook. Cook just a few at a time so you don't overcrowd the pan and lower the temperature of the oil. When they are golden brown (after 2–3 minutes), use the slotted spoon to transfer them to paper towels to drain. Repeat to cook the remaining florets. Serve the warm pakoras with raita.

BUCKWHEAT PANCAKES

WITH BLUEBERRY MAPLE GLAZE AND CINNAMON BUTTER

These delicious pancakes never fail to impress my friends and family, and the cinnamon butter tops them off beautifully.

Serves 2–3

45 g (1¾ oz/⅓ cup) buckwheat flour
   (see helpful hint)
50 g (1¾ oz/⅓ cup) self-raising flour
1 teaspoon baking powder
1 tablespoon caster
   (superfine) sugar
1 egg, lightly whisked
160 ml (5¼ fl oz/⅔ cup) milk
40 g (1½ oz) butter

BLUEBERRY MAPLE GLAZE

155 g (5½ oz/1 cup) fresh
   blueberries
2 tablespoons maple syrup
1 teaspoon caster (superfine) sugar

CINNAMON BUTTER

50 g (1¾ oz) butter, at room
   temperature
1 teaspoon ground cinnamon

1 Sift the flours, baking powder and sugar into a large mixing bowl. Make a well (a small hole) in the centre and add the egg. Whisk to combine, then while whisking constantly, slowly pour in the milk. Whisk until there are no lumps, then set aside for 15 minutes.

2 Meanwhile, to make the blueberry maple glaze, put the blueberries, maple syrup and sugar in a small saucepan over low heat. Cook, stirring, for 4–5 minutes or until the sugar has dissolved and the berries start to break down. Remove from the heat.

3 To make the cinnamon butter, use a fork to mash the butter and cinnamon until combined. Place on plastic wrap, shape into

a log and wrap up to enclose, twisting the ends. Roll the log along the bench to make a nice, neat shape. Refrigerate until firm. Just before serving, unwrap and slice into rounds.

4 Heat half the butter in a large non-stick frying over medium heat. Using a ladle or jug, pour 60 ml (2 fl oz/¼ cup) quantities of the pancake batter into the pan, to make 2 or 3 pancakes. Cook until bubbles begin to appear on the surface, then turn and cook for 30 seconds on the other side. Transfer to a plate and cover loosely with foil to keep warm. Repeat with the remaining batter. Serve the pancakes with the blueberry maple glaze and cinnamon butter.

RICOTTA DUMPLINGS

WITH ORANGE SUGAR

Makes about 20

2 free-range eggs
80 g (2¾ oz) caster (superfine) sugar
150 g (5½ oz/1 cup) plain
   (all-purpose) flour
2 teaspoons baking powder
finely grated zest of 1 large orange
350 g (12 oz) fresh ricotta cheese
vegetable oil, for deep-frying
30 g (1 oz/¼ cup) icing
   (confectioners') sugar, sifted

HELPFUL HINT

A good way to test if the oil is hot enough is to stick the end of a wooden spoon in it. If the oil starts to bubble about the wood, it is ready.

1 Use an electric mixer to beat the eggs and sugar in a large mixing bowl until thick and pale. Sift the flour and baking powder together.

2 Add half the orange zest and the ricotta to the egg mixture and use a spatula to fold together. Add the flour mixture and stir until well combined. You should have a wet-looking dough.

3 Pour enough oil into a medium saucepan to come halfway up the side of the pan. Heat over low heat until the oil reaches 180°C (350°F) or a cube of bread dropped into the oil turns golden brown in 15 seconds (see helpful hint). (See the safety tips for frying on page 11.)

4 Spoon 2–3 tablespoons of the batter, one at a time, into the hot oil and fry the dumplings, turning to ensure they brown evenly, for 3–4 minutes or until puffed and golden. Use a slotted spoon to transfer to paper towels to drain. Repeat to cook the remaining dumplings. Mix together the remaining orange zest and the icing sugar and dust over the dumplings. Serve warm.

CHILL

EQUIPMENT

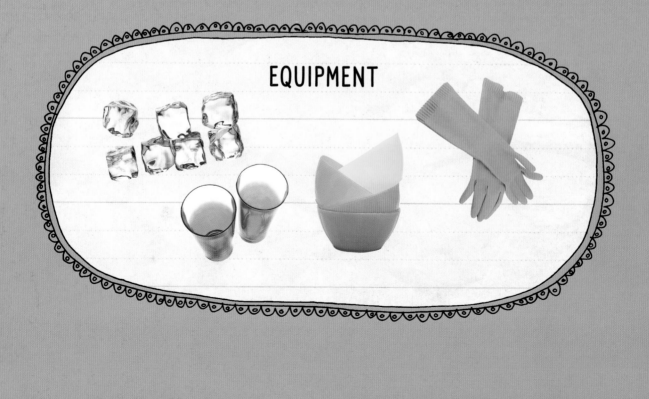

Smoothies, sorbets, ice creams and dips should always be served at the correct temperature, which is usually chilled or frozen. When it is time to cool dishes in a refrigerator or allow them to set in a freezer, you need to be patient. You may be hungry and tempted to stick your little finger in, but please don't! I promise the results will be worth the wait. Ice cubes are often required in this chapter, so check your supply the day before you want to cook one of these refreshing chilled recipes.

GUACAMOLE

WITH FRESH SALSA

Serves 4–6

2 ripe avocados, halved and
   stones removed
2 limes
1 small red onion, finely chopped
1 tablespoon sour cream
10 cherry tomatoes, quartered
½ long red chilli, seeded and finely
   chopped (see helpful hint)
¼ cup coriander (cilantro) leaves,
   coarsely chopped
oven-baked tortilla chips (slice soft
   tortillas and crimp them slightly,
   then bake until lightly browned)
   or vegetable sticks, to serve

1 Spoon the avocado flesh into a medium mixing bowl and mash with a fork. Add the juice of 1 lime, half the onion, the sour cream, a good pinch of salt and some freshly ground black pepper. Stir to combine, then place in a serving dish. Refrigerate until ready to serve.

2 Combine the tomatoes, chilli, remaining onion and the coriander in a small mixing bowl. Add the juice of the remaining lime and a pinch of salt. Pile over the guacamole and serve with tortilla chips or vegetable sticks.

HELPFUL HINT
Wear disposable or rubber
gloves when handling chillies,
to avoid getting capsaicin
(which is responsible for the
heat) on your hands as you may
rub your eyes or put them
in your mouth afterwards.

HELPFUL HINT
The juice from beetroot can stain your fingers and clothes, so wear rubber gloves or wash your hands with warm water straight after handling them.

BEETROOT TZATZIKI

Dips are a great healthy snack, perfect to put in a lunch box with vegetable sticks or pull out of the fridge when friends drop in. There are loads of flavour combinations you can try, so experiment with whatever is in season. I usually serve my dips with toasted pitta bread, celery or carrot sticks.

Serves 4–6

2 medium beetroot (beets),
    peeled (see helpful hint)
260 g (9¼ oz/1 cup) Greek-style
    yoghurt
1 garlic clove, crushed
1 teaspoon salt

1 Cook the beetroot in a medium saucepan of boiling water for 30 minutes or until tender (insert a skewer into the beetroot to test their tenderness). Drain and place in a bowl of cold water for 10 minutes or until cool. Drain well, then coarsely grate.

2 Combine the grated beetroot, yoghurt, garlic and salt in a medium mixing bowl. Stir well to combine. Cover and refrigerate until ready to serve.

FRESH HUMMUS

Serves 4–6

400 g (14 oz) tin organic chickpeas,
    drained and rinsed
1 garlic clove, crushed
1 teaspoon tahini
1 lemon, juiced, plus 1 lemon
    wedge, to serve
1 teaspoon sea salt
2 tablespoons olive oil
pinch of sweet paprika

1 Put the chickpeas, garlic, tahini, lemon juice, salt and half the oil in a food processor and process until combined. The mixture will be a little thick, so gradually add a dash of water until it is a smooth consistency. Cover and refrigerate until ready to serve.

2 Serve drizzled with the remaining oil, sprinkled with paprika and with a lemon wedge squeezed over.

RAITA

This is a great side dish for curries and other spicy dishes. It is fresh and cooling, so it soothes the mouth after eating a hot dish. I also like to serve it as a dip with flatbread.

Serves 4–6

350 g (12 oz) Greek-style
   pot set yoghurt
300 g (10½ oz) Lebanese (short)
   cucumber, grated and excess
   liquid squeezed out
1 teaspoon sea salt
1 tablespoon coarsely chopped
   mint (or coriander/cilantro)

1 Line a bowl with a large piece of muslin (cheesecloth; see helpful hint) or a clean tea towel (dish towel). Spoon the yoghurt into the cloth and twist the ends tightly to form a ball, then secure the top with an elastic band.

2 Hang the yoghurt bundle above a sink or over a bowl for at least 1 hour. The excess liquid from the yoghurt will drip through the cloth, leaving you with a lovely thick yoghurt.

3 Put the drained yoghurt in a large mixing bowl. Add the cucumber, salt and mint and stir well to combine. Cover and refrigerate until ready to serve.

HELPFUL HINT
Muslin is a thin cloth
material with very fine
holes, available from
kitchenware stores.

THE ULTIMATE BANANA SPLIT

This delicious retro dessert can be whipped up in a flash, so store it in your memory bank. The rich chocolate ganache is a handy recipe, as it can be used in other dessert recipes or you can simply serve it over ice cream for an indulgent after-dinner treat.

Serves 4

4 firm ripe bananas, peeled
20 g (¾ oz) unsalted butter
1 teaspoon light brown sugar
8 small scoops vanilla ice cream
50 g (1¾ oz) slivered almonds,
   lightly toasted

CHOCOLATE GANACHE

80 ml (2½ fl oz/⅓ cup) thin
   (pouring/whipping) cream
20 g (¾ oz) unsalted butter
190 g (6¾ oz) dark chocolate,
   finely chopped

1 To make the chocolate ganache, heat the cream and butter in a small saucepan over low heat until just below boiling point (small bubbles will start to form around the edge of the pan). Put the chocolate in a heatproof bowl, pour over the hot cream mixture and use a spatula to stir until the chocolate has melted and the mixture is smooth and glossy. This will take a few minutes.

2 Cut the bananas in half lengthways, then in half widthways. Heat the butter in a medium frying pan over medium–high heat, add the sugar and cook, stirring, for 30 seconds. Add the bananas, cut side down, and cook for 2–3 minutes or until caramelised. Remove from the heat.

3 Divide the warm bananas and ice cream among serving dishes. Drizzle with the chocolate ganache and sprinkle with almonds. Serve immediately.

HELPFUL HINT
If you want to play around with the recipe a little, try substituting caramel sauce for the chocolate ganache.

CHEAT'S CHEESECAKES

WITH BLACKBERRIES AND TOASTED ALMONDS

The only cooking these quick and easy cheesecakes require is melting butter in the microwave. They can be made ahead and stored in the refrigerator until needed. Making them in short, wide individual glasses means you can admire the layers, but you can make one large portion if you prefer.

Serves 4

60 g (2¼ oz) unsalted butter

120 g (4¼ oz) gingernut or digestive biscuits, roughly crushed

finely grated zest of 1 lemon

200 g (7 oz) mascarpone cheese (see helpful hint)

1 tablespoon thin (pouring/ whipping) cream

1 tablespoon caster (superfine) sugar

125 g (4½ oz) fresh blackberries

30 g (1 oz) slivered almonds, lightly toasted

1 Put the butter in a microwave-safe bowl, cover with plastic wrap and microwave on medium (50%) for 1 minute or until melted. (The time can vary depending on your microwave.) Put the crushed biscuits in a mixing bowl, pour over the melted butter and stir to combine. Divide the biscuit mixture among four 250 ml (9 fl oz/1 cup) serving glasses.

2 Put the lemon zest, mascarpone, cream and sugar in a medium mixing bowl and use an electric mixer to beat until smooth and slightly thickened. Add a heaped spoonful or two of the cream mixture to each glass. Top with a few blackberries, scatter with the almonds and serve.

HELPFUL HINT

Mascarpone is an Italian cream cheese that is available from supermarkets. It has a mild taste and carries flavour, such as citrus zest, very well. It is often used in desserts, but also works well in savoury dishes such as risotto.

PUDDING CAKE 'N' CUSTARD

This heavenly combination is just the thing for an afternoon tea or dessert cake. You can also flavour the custard with finely grated orange zest instead of vanilla.

Serves 10

PUDDING CAKE

250 g (9 oz/1⅔ cups) plain
  (all-purpose) flour
1 teaspoon baking powder
½ teaspoon bicarbonate of soda
  (baking soda)
½ teaspoon salt
125 g (4½ oz) unsalted butter,
  chopped and softened
220 g (7¾ oz/1 cup) caster
  (superfine) sugar
3 free-range eggs
finely grated zest of 1 orange
200 ml (7 fl oz) buttermilk

CUSTARD

250 ml (9 fl oz/1 cup) thin (pouring/
  whipping) cream
250 ml (9 fl oz/1 cup) milk
1 vanilla bean, split lengthways
  and seeds scraped (see helpful
  hint on page 153)
6 large free-range egg yolks
100 g (3½ oz) caster (superfine)
  sugar

1 Preheat the oven to 180°C (350°F/Gas 4). Grease a round 20 cm (8 inch) cake tin and line with non-stick baking paper.

2 Sift the flour, baking powder, bicarbonate of soda and salt together. Use an electric mixer to beat the butter and sugar in a large bowl until pale and creamy. Add the eggs one at a time, beating on low speed after each addition until well combined. Mix in the orange zest.

3 Stir in the flour mixture alternately with the buttermilk, in 2–3 batches each, stirring until well combined. Spoon into the prepared tin. Bake for 40–45 minutes or until light golden and a skewer inserted in the centre of the cake comes out clean. Transfer to a wire rack and set aside for 10 minutes to cool, then remove the tin and baking paper.

4 Meanwhile, to make the custard, heat the cream, milk and vanilla seeds and pod in a medium saucepan over low heat. Bring to just below boiling point (small bubbles will start to form around the edges), then remove from the heat. Set aside to cool.

5 Use an electric mixer to beat the egg yolks and sugar in a medium bowl until pale. Whisk in the cooled milk mixture, then strain through a sieve into a medium saucepan. Cook over low heat, stirring constantly with a wooden spoon, until the custard thickens slightly. Remove from the heat. Serve with slices of warm pudding cake.

HELPFUL HINT
The custard will keep
in an airtight container
in the fridge for
up to 2 days.

SHAKE

EQUIPMENT

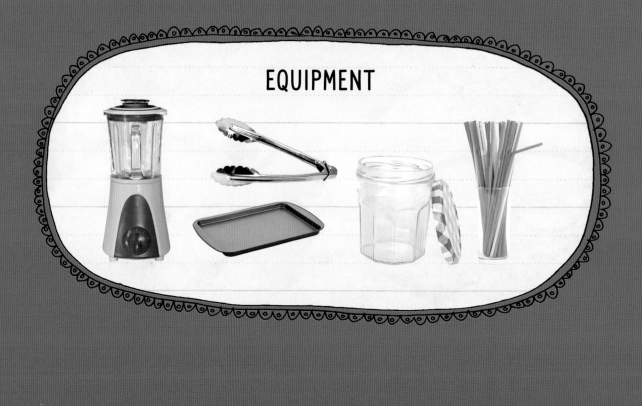

This chapter is all about using your hands. The recipes require blending, shaking, mixing, rubbing, coating or seasoning. When it comes to the 'shake', I encourage the use of large snap-lock bags, a good blender and some clean jars with screw-top lids. The best trick I've learnt in the kitchen is combining my dressing ingredients in a jar and giving it a good old shake. That way you know your ingredients are combined well and if you have any leftovers, you can put them straight in the fridge. Dressings will generally keep for about a week or two.

NO-FUSS LAMB CUTLETS

WITH ZESTY TOMATO SALSA

Serves 4

2 garlic cloves, crushed

1 tablespoon finely chopped
   flat-leaf (Italian) parsley

2 tablespoons olive oil

8 lamb cutlets, french trimmed
   (see helpful hint)

pan-fried halved baby zucchini
   (courgettes), to serve

TOMATO SALSA

2 tablespoons coarsely chopped
   coriander (cilantro)

2 vine-ripened tomatoes,
   coarsely chopped

½ red capsicum (pepper), seeded
   and coarsely chopped

juice of 1 lime

1 teaspoon caster (superfine) sugar

50 g (1¾ oz/¼ cup) freshly cooked
   corn kernels

1 spring onion (scallion), trimmed
   and thinly sliced

1 Put the garlic, parsley, oil and some salt and pepper in a large snap-lock bag (it needs to hold all the cutlets). Add the cutlets, seal the bag and give a good shake, until all the cutlets are coated in the marinade. Refrigerate for at least 30 minutes to marinate.

2 Meanwhile, to make the tomato salsa, combine all the ingredients in a medium mixing bowl and season with salt. Set aside (do not refrigerate).

3 Heat a large frying pan over high heat and cook the lamb cutlets, in batches, for 2–3 minutes each side. Serve the cutlets with the tomato salsa and the zucchini.

HELPFUL HINT
French-trimmed meat
has had the top of the
bones scraped to remove
any fat, sinew or meat,
making it look neater
once cooked.

SALAD DRESSINGS

Behind every great salad there has to be a great dressing. To make these tasty, zesty dressings, put all the ingredients in a clean jar with a screw-top lid and shake lightly before pouring over the salad. Always use good-quality extra virgin olive oil — since you are not cooking with it, the flavour can really be appreciated and will bring your dressings to life.

DIJON DRESSING

A great all-round dressing that is particularly good with salads that have beef or chicken in them.

Makes 100 ml (3½ fl oz)

1 teaspoon dijon mustard
60 ml (2 fl oz/¼ cup) extra virgin olive oil
juice of ½ lemon
1 small garlic clove, crushed
1 teaspoon caster (superfine) sugar
salt and pepper

ORANGE AND SESAME DRESSING

This dressing has a subtle sweetness that is fantastic with Asian-style salads.

Makes 90 ml (3 fl oz)

1 teaspoon honey
1 teaspoon dijon mustard
2 tablespoons freshly squeezed
   orange juice
2 tablespoons olive oil
a few drops of sesame oil
1 teaspoon sesame seeds
salt and pepper

TANGY YOGHURT DRESSING

This thick dressing is great with spinach, iceberg lettuce and spring onion (scallion). Add chicken or lamb for a heartier meal.

Makes 175 ml (5½ fl oz)

80 g (2¾ oz) Greek-style yoghurt
juice of 1 lemon
1 garlic clove, crushed
1 tablespoon olive oil
½ teaspoon caster (superfine) sugar
1 teaspoon ground coriander
1 teaspoon ground cumin
½ teaspoon sweet paprika (optional)
salt and pepper

BALSAMIC DRESSING

This is a staple of mine, as it can be put on just about anything.

Makes 100 ml (3½ fl oz)

1 tablespoon balsamic vinegar
80 ml (2½ fl oz/⅓ cup) extra virgin olive oil
½ teaspoon caster (superfine) sugar
1 small garlic clove, crushed (optional)
salt and pepper

CINNAMON CHICKEN DRUMETTES

Serves 4

2 garlic cloves, crushed
80 ml (2½ fl oz/⅓ cup) lemon juice
½ teaspoon ground cumin
1½ teaspoons ground cinnamon
390 g (13¾ oz/1½ cups) Greek-style
   yoghurt
1 kg (2 lb 4 oz) chicken drumettes
1 tablespoon olive oil
salad leaves and lemon wedges,
   to serve

1 Combine the garlic, lemon juice, cumin, cinnamon, yoghurt and a good pinch of salt in a large glass or ceramic bowl. Add the chicken drumettes, cover with plastic wrap and gently shake the bowl to coat the chicken in the marinade. Refrigerate for at least 1 hour.

2 Heat the oil in a large frying pan over medium heat. Shake any excess marinade off the drumettes and cook, in batches, for 4–5 minutes each side or until golden brown and cooked through. Serve the drumettes with salad leaves and lemon wedges.

GARLIC AND CITRUS PRAWNS

Serves 4

12–16 large raw prawns (shrimp)
2 tablespoons olive oil
½ teaspoon sesame oil
3 garlic cloves, crushed
1 teaspoon sea salt
½ long red chilli, seeded and
   finely chopped
finely grated zest of 1 lime
1 large lemon, zest finely grated
mixed salad, to serve

1 Peel and devein the prawns, removing the shells and leaving the tails on. Put the prawns in a large snap-lock bag with the olive oil, sesame oil, garlic, salt and chilli. Seal the bag and shake to coat the prawns evenly in the mixture. Refrigerate for at least 1 hour or overnight to marinate.

2 Open the bag and add the lime and lemon zest to the prawns, then seal again and shake to combine. Heat a large char-grill pan or barbecue plate on high heat. Cook the prawns for 1–2 minutes each side or until they are lightly charred and cooked through (they will turn opaque). Transfer to a serving dish. Cut the lemon in half and squeeze the juice over the prawns. Serve with the mixed salad.

HONEYED PARSNIPS AND CARROTS

WITH THYME

When I was a child I was quite a fussy eater and only ate vegetables that were presented plainly on the plate. How silly I was! My students absolutely love this recipe — the magic ingredients of honey, thyme and butter are a lovely combination. Goodbye, bland vegetables!

Serves 6

6 carrots, peeled
6 parsnips, peeled
50 g (1¾ oz) butter, chopped
2 tablespoons thyme leaves,
  finely chopped
1 heaped tablespoon honey
1 tablespoon olive oil
1 teaspoon sesame seeds

1 Preheat the oven to 210°C (415°F/Gas 6–7). Cut the vegetables in half lengthways, then into quarters so they look like long chips. Put them in a large microwave-oven steamer bag. Add the butter, thyme, honey, a good pinch of salt and some pepper. Seal the bag and shake well to mix all the ingredients together.

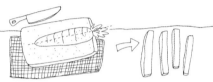

2 Cook the vegetables in the microwave on medium–high heat (70-80%) for 2 minutes. Carefully remove the bag and shake again.

3 Tip the vegetables out into a large roasting pan. Drizzle with oil, sprinkle with sesame seeds and bake for 35–40 minutes. They will be caramelised (sweet) and golden, with a nice crunch.

BLUEBERRY MILKSHAKE

WITH A TWIST

**A bit of this and a touch of that makes nothing short of the perfect shake!
I get cravings for cool and creamy shakes such as this.**

Serves 2

155 g (5½ oz/1 cup) fresh
  blueberries
250 ml (9 fl oz/1 cup) milk
1 teaspoon honey
pinch of ground cinnamon
2 tablespoons plain yoghurt
2 passionfruit, halved

1 Put the blueberries, milk, honey, cinnamon and yoghurt in a blender and blend until smooth. Pour into glasses and scoop the passionfruit pulp over the top. Serve immediately.

People who know what is naturally good for their bodies have a huge advantage over those who don't. A balanced diet that is full of variety combined with lots of fresh air, physical exercise and clean water to drink boosts our chances of a long and happy life, free of illness and disease. These days, a vast number of foods are packaged and processed. I have spoken to children who thought peas grew in a freezer bag! If we don't know where food comes from, how can we know what is going into our bodies and whether it is good or bad for us? Choosing seasonal produce and planting a veggie patch (however small) allows us to control the good stuff. Learning how to grow food is fascinating and fun, and also encourages a healthy environment and sustainable living. I believe that understanding and connecting with food from a young age sets us on the path to health and happiness.

Abraham, 11

LOOKING AFTER YOUR BODY

Nutrition and health are made up of a number of contributing factors, all of which affect our lives. These include the foods we eat, the water we drink, and exercise. We all have different food requirements and these change as we get older. For example, a competitive athlete will need a higher energy intake than an everyday person doing normal activities.

The Dietary Guidelines for Children and Adolescents in Australia recommend children and adolescents eat plenty of vegetables, fruits, legumes and cereals (preferably wholegrain, and including bread, rice, pasta and noodles). Lean meat, fish, poultry, milks, yoghurt and cheeses should also be included. The drink of choice should be water, and lots of it.

Variety is also important for a balanced diet. In my role as a teacher, I regularly witness children trying new foods — they appreciate and understand the Kitchen Garden philosophy and know why it is important for healthy living. I build menus that embrace new foods and different cultures. We learn to experience variety and balance in our diets. I love seeing the enthusiasm in my students' faces when we explore a completely new food, especially if they have watched it grow from seed. There is genuine interest in its journey.

Andrew, 10

Prasanna, 10

BE CREATIVE AND EXPLORE

The wonderful world of food is an exciting area to explore. Understanding where our food comes from and knowing how to prepare fresh, seasonal and tasty meals ourselves is an important part of a healthy lifestyle. Schools are now taking a smart approach to food, creating kitchen garden and healthy eating programs encouraging students to make positive food choices. Whether it's growing, buying or cooking your own food, it should be fun, not a chore. Here are some suggestions you might like to try to ensure cooking is part of your everyday life.

- Challenge your tastebuds. Our tastes continue to change and evolve as we grow. What we found tasty and ate when we were babies changes (thank goodness!) — new likes and dislikes form.

- Try something new. Be creative with your cooking and try a variety of different ingredients on a regular basis. I like to encourage my students to try at least one new fruit or vegetable every week.

- Make a recipe your own. Don't be afraid to change and adapt recipes to suit your own tastes. This is a great way to explore a variety of foods and gives you a chance to change your mind.

- Write your own menus. Devise a seasonal menu to cook and enjoy with your family and friends.

- Plant your own herb or vegetable garden. Do this at home if you can, or suggest it to your teacher. Nominate an area within the school for a small edible garden and rally students, parents and teachers to get involved. A kitchen garden is a great educational resource.

- Set up a community garden. Talk to your neighbours and approach your local council about assigning a portion of land to create a community garden. It will be close to home and is a convenient, healthy way to get food. Many communities are taking these opportunities, as they can see the benefits for both themselves and the environment.

- Visit your local farmers' market, fresh food market or community garden. They are becoming much more common, so you may well have one nearby. Do a search on the internet or call your local council to locate the nearest one. They are a fabulous way to explore and understand seasonal, home-grown and organic produce.

- Chat to farmers and gardeners. Learn where specific produce has come from and how it has been grown or treated.

ACKNOWLEDGMENTS

I begin with my amazing and truly inspiring parents, Ross and Virginia, who continually encourage me to achieve and succeed. My mother is a wonderful English teacher and together we share a love for education. She has listened, loved and supported me through everything and if it wasn't for her, I would talk over absolutely everyone! To my father, who is passionate about fine produce supported by local people — I really appreciate the growing connection to food we are exploring together. Thank you to my beautiful sisters Edwina and Amelia, who are my heart, head and happiness through everything. Thank you also to my informative and ever-expanding food network of work colleagues, friends, families and farmers.

Dearest Daniel, Holly and the whole team at Murdoch Books. Thank you for believing in me and knowing what I'm capable of.

I wish to thank my Murdoch publishers Anneka Manning and Sally Webb, my editor Anna Scobie and project manager Laura Wilson for helping my words come to life. Thank you to my photographers Alicia Taylor and Tim de Neefe, food stylist Sarah de Nardi and home economist on the photo shoot Caroline Jones. Special thanks also to my food editor Chrissy Freer. A big thank you to my enthusiastic and talented illustrator Dawn Tan — together I think we've created a visually stunning book appropriate for children of all ages.

A big thank you to the students, parents and staff of Findon Primary School for opening their minds and allowing me to share, explore, learn and grow with them. I also wish to thank Stephanie Alexander and The Foundation for their support of my first cookbook and their valuable work with primary school children.

Finally, and most importantly, thank you to my beloved Harry and Frankie, who help me see the world through loving eyes...

INDEX